AF471033

BUSES IN CAMERA: North-West

Dwarfed by the bulk of Widnes
Transporter Bridge, this Massey-bodied Leyland Titan
TD4 (No 43 – BTD 124) was one of a batch of five placed
in service by Widnes Corporation in 1936.
Leyland Vehicles

BUSES IN CAMERA:
North - West

John P. Robinson

LONDON
IAN ALLAN LTD

Contents

First published 1985

ISBN 0 7110 1489 2

© Ian Allan Ltd 1985

Published by Ian Allan Ltd, Shepperton, Surrey; and printed by Ian Allan Printing Ltd at their works at Coombelands in Runnymede, England.

The damp and dismal atmosphere of Salford's Greengate terminus, located in the arches beneath the now closed Manchester Exchange station, has changed little over the years. Two Greater Manchester Transport standard double-deckers, a Daimler Fleetline (nearest) and a Leyland Atlantean, are depicted there on 13 March 1984. *John Robinson*

Introduction

Taking the North Western Traffic Area as its scope, this book sets out to project, principally with photographs, something of the character of Public Service Vehicle operations in this part of the country over the last 50 years. The area covered comprises Cheshire, Lancashire (apart from the Bowland District of North Lancashire which came under the Yorkshire Traffic Area), Greater Manchester, Merseyside, the High Peak District of Derbyshire and North Wales (embracing the 'old' counties of Anglesey, Caernarvon, Denbigh, Flint, Merionethshire and Montgomery).

Given the extent of the area, its geographical diversity and the large number of operators based within it, such a task is a formidable one indeed, and it has not been possible to cover all the aspects of potential interest within the space available.

Not unnaturally, the photographs presented are very much a personal choice, although a deliberate attempt has been made to depict as wide a range of types as possible so that, for example, the Bolton Corporation photographs are of AEC, Crossley, Leyland and Daimler chassis bodied by Metro-Cammell, Crossley, Bond and East Lancashire respectively. Whilst it has not been practicable to sustain this approach with every operator, the emphasis on variety is maintained throughout the book.

If there is a slight preponderance of Leylands this is only because, quite understandably, the marque has always predominated in most parts of the area covered. Many operators bought no other make, year after year, the classic example being Preston Corporation (now Borough of Preston) Transport Department, all but three of the buses purchased since 1922, when motorbus operations com-menced, until the present day, being Leylands. Other undertakings displayed similar loyalty to local manufacturers – Manchester and Stockport with Crossley, Blackburn (in later years at least) with the town's bodybuilder, East Lancashire, and Wigan with the two local bodybuilding concerns of Massey and Northern Counties, to give just a few examples. Of course, not all undertakings bought locally, a case in point being Morecambe & Heysham Corporation, whose fleet had a rather 'southern' character, for many years standardising on AEC Regents with Park Royal or Weymann bodywork.

On 1 April 1984 the number of Traffic Areas was reduced from 11 to nine and some changes were made to their boundaries. The North Western Traffic Area lost the Montgomery District of Powys to the South Wales Traffic Area, with which it undoubtedly had more affinity, at the same time gaining Cumbria from the Northern Traffic Area and the Bowland District of Lancashire. With space at a premium it was decided, however, not to provide coverage of these additional areas, the principal operators in which are Barrow-in-Furness Transport and NBC subsidiary Cumberland Motor Services Ltd.

Most of the illustrations used have not previously been published, and I extend my thanks to the photographers concerned. Special mention must be made of Roy Marshall and Mike Taylor who, in addition to providing some excellent photographs, furnished me with details of some of the buses which were 'before my time', and also Simon Forty for his assistance in this compilation.

John Robinson

Municipal Undertakings and PTEs

No fewer than 33 municipal transport undertakings were located in the North Western Traffic Area until 1968. By far the greatest concentration of these was in Lancashire, which was a complexity of separate systems within which a great deal of joint operation evolved. The area agreement companies – Crosville, North Western and Ribble – together with independent Lancashire United were parties to this, in addition to the municipals themselves.

For the purposes of this book municipal operators are grouped into six sections:

East Lancashire
Accrington Corporation Transport Department
Blackburn Corporation Transport Department
Burnley, Colne & Nelson Joint Transport Committee
Darwen Corporation Transport Department
Haslingden Corporation Transport Department
Rawtenstall Corporation Motors

Preston and the Fylde coast
Preston Corporation Transport Department
Lytham St Annes Corporation Transport Department
Blackpool Corporation Transport

Lancaster and Morecambe Bay
Lancaster City Transport
Morecambe & Heysham Corporation Transport Department

Cheshire and North Wales
Chester City Transport
Colwyn Bay Borough Council
Llandudno Urban District Council
Warrington Corporation Transport Department
Widnes Corporation Transport Department

SELNEC PTE – Constituent fleets
Ashton-under-Lyne Corporation Passenger Transport
Bolton (County Borough of) Transport Department
Bury Corporation Transport
Leigh Corporation Transport
Manchester City Transport Department
Oldham Corporation Passenger Transport Department
Ramsbottom UDC Transport Department
Rochdale Corporation Transport Department
Salford City Transport
Stalybridge, Hyde, Mossley & Dukinfield Joint Transport & Electricity Board
Stockport Corporation Transport Department
Wigan Corporation Transport Department

Merseyside PTE – Constituent fleets
Birkenhead Corporation Transport Department
Liverpool Corporation Passenger Transport
St Helens Corporation Transport
Southport Corporation Transport Department
Wallasey Corporation Motor Buses

Although vehicle designs have been the subject of continual change, with radical developments being made after, and in part due to, the 1939-45 war, little happened to the structure of the bus industry after the enactment of the Road Traffic Act in 1930 until the end of the 1960s.

The 1968 Transport Act decreed the setting up of the National Bus Company (NBC) and the Passenger Transport Executives (PTEs); out of the four original PTEs two, Merseyside and SELNEC (South East Lancashire North East Cheshire) were in the North West, centred on the two principal cities of Liverpool and Manchester. Between them these two infant operators absorbed no fewer than 14 municipal undertakings, ranging in size from the massive Liverpool and Manchester, both of which had fleets exceeding 1,000, to the tiny Ramsbottom, with a mere 13 vehicles. The strong sense of individuality carefully built up over the years by each of these undertakings was at an end; their distinctive liveries gradually disappeared, to be replaced, most would agree, by anonymous corporate liveries. Simplicity of application, ease of maintenance and low cost were the ruling factors, and liveries such as Ashton-under-Lyne's superb Peacock Blue and Cream were incompatible with these objectives.

The reorganisation of local government in 1974 depressed the ranks of the area's municipal

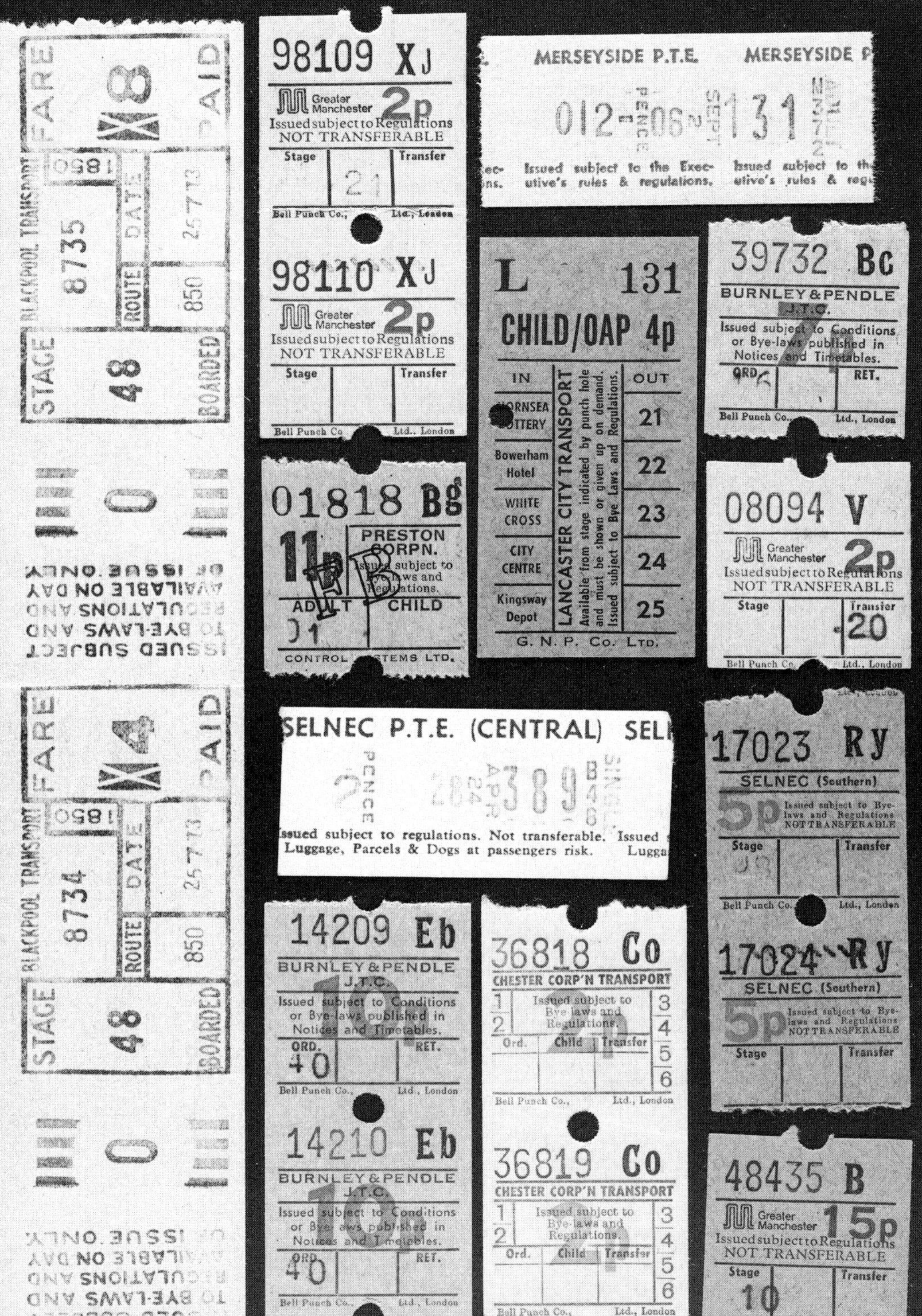
FARE 8 X
BLACKPOOL TRANSPORT
8735
1850
ROUTE DATE 25 7 73
850
STAGE 48
BOARDED
PAID
0
AVAILABLE ON DAY OF ISSUE ONLY.
REGULATIONS AND
ISSUED SUBJECT TO BYE-LAWS AND
FARE 4 X
BLACKPOOL TRANSPORT
8734
1850
ROUTE DATE 25 7 73
850
STAGE 48
BOARDED
PAID
0
AVAILABLE ON DAY OF ISSUE ONLY.
REGULATIONS AND
ISSUED SUBJECT TO BYE-LAWS AND
98109 XJ
Greater Manchester 2p
Issued subject to Regulations
NOT TRANSFERABLE
Stage Transfer
21
Bell Punch Co. Ltd., London
98110 XJ
Greater Manchester 2p
Issued subject to Regulations
NOT TRANSFERABLE
Stage Transfer
Bell Punch Co Ltd., London
01818 Bg
11p PRESTON CORPN.
Issued subject to Bye-laws and Regulations.
ADULT CHILD
01
CONTROL SYSTEMS LTD.
SELNEC P.T.E. (CENTRAL) SEL
2 PENCE
APR 28
389
Issued subject to regulations. Not transferable. Issued
Luggage, Parcels & Dogs at passengers risk. Lugga
14209 Eb
BURNLEY & PENDLE J.T.C.
Issued subject to Conditions or Bye-laws published in Notices and Timetables.
ORD. 40 RET.
Bell Punch Co. Ltd., London
14210 Eb
BURNLEY & PENDLE J.T.C.
Issued subject to Conditions or Bye-laws published in Notices and Timetables.
ORD. 40 RET.
Bell Punch Co. Ltd., London
MERSEYSIDE P.T.E. MERSEYSIDE P
012 210 131
SEPT 2 90
PENCE
Issued subject to the Exec-utive's rules & regulations.
Issued subject to th utive's rules & regu
L 131
CHILD/OAP 4p
LANCASTER CITY TRANSPORT
IN OUT
HORNSEA POTTERY 21
Bowerham Hotel 22
WHITE CROSS 23
CITY CENTRE 24
Kingsway Depot 25
Available from stage indicated by punch hole and must be shown or given up on demand. Issued subject to Bye-laws and Regulations.
G. N. P. Co. Ltd.
36818 Co
CHESTER CORP'N TRANSPORT
1 2 Issued subject to Bye-laws and Regulations. 3 4
Ord. Child Transfer 5 6
Bell Punch Co., Ltd., London
36819 Co
CHESTER CORP'N TRANSPORT
1 2 Issued subject to Bye-laws and Regulations. 3 4
Ord. Child Transfer 5 6
Bell Punch Co., Ltd., London
39732 Bc
BURNLEY & PENDLE J.T.C.
Issued subject to Conditions or Bye-laws published in Notices and Timetables.
ORD. RET.
Bell Punch Co. Ltd., London
08094 V
Greater Manchester 2p
Issued subject to Regulations
NOT TRANSFERABLE
Stage Transfer
20
Bell Punch Co. Ltd., London
17023 Ry
SELNEC (Southern)
5p Issued subject to Bye-laws and Regulations NOT TRANSFERABLE
Stage Transfer
Bell Punch Co. Ltd., London
17024 Ry
SELNEC (Southern)
5p Issued subject to Bye-laws and Regulations NOT TRANSFERABLE
Stage Transfer
48435 B
Greater Manchester 15p
Issued subject to Regulations
NOT TRANSFERABLE
Stage Transfer
10
Bell Punch Co. Ltd., London

undertakings even further. The formation of the new Metropolitan Counties of Merseyside and Greater Manchester accounted for the absorption of the St Helens and Southport fleets into the enlarged Merseyside PTE, whilst SELNEC was rechristened Greater Manchester PTE and absorbed Wigan Corporation Transport, which fell within the new Greater Manchester County. At the same time the Blackburn and Darwen, and Lancaster and Morecambe & Heysham undertakings were merged, each taking their title from the former operator, whilst a number of other undertakings were re-named; Accrington becoming Hyndburn, Burnley, Colne & Nelson becoming Burnley & Pendle, Lytham becoming Fylde, Colwyn Bay becoming Colwyn, Llandudno becoming Aberconwy and Widnes becoming Halton.

Remembering that Rawtenstall and its somewhat smaller neighbour, Haslingden, which had both been under the same General Manager for some years, were merged to form the Rossendale Joint Transport Committe in 1968, the number of municipal undertakings in the North Western Traffic Area had been reduced to just 13 in 1974, a figure which still stands, although only just, for in 1982 Fylde was in danger of being taken over by its larger neighbour, Blackpool, although its future existence now seems more secure.

EAST LANCASHIRE

Accrington

Above: Four handsome Roberts-bodied Daimler CVD6s were placed in service by Accrington in 1949. No 124, the second vehicle of the batch, stands ahead of No 3 (JTF 739), a Burlingham-bodied Leyland Tiger PS1 new the previous year. *Roy Marshall*

Right: Accrington became quite a keen operator of Guys after the war; No 14 was one of three Guy Arab LUFs delivered in 1956, with East Lancashire 43-seat rear-entrance bodywork. *Roy Marshall*

Above: Depicted turning out of Accrington bus station, No 22 was one of eight Leyland Tiger Cubs with East Lancashire bodywork placed in service between 1962 and 1965. On the right, loading for Oswaldtwistle, is No 147 (388 FTB), an East Lancashire-bodied Guy Arab IV dating from 1958. *T. W. Moore*

Below: Accrington, and its successor Hyndburn, standardised on East Lancashire-bodied Leyland Atlanteans for its double-deck fleet between 1969 and 1980, a total of 29 being purchased. No 198, one of the last pair delivered, is depicted at the undertaking's Ellison Street garage on 18 February 1984, wearing the predominantly white overall advertising livery for the Red Rose Rambler ticket, promoted by Lancashire County Council in conjunction with all the major bus operators in the county, each of which had a bus similarly adorned. *John Robinson*

Blackburn

Above: Leyland buses were purchased almost exclusively by Blackburn Corporation from 1929 until the arrival of utility Guy Arabs. No 33 (BV 1070), a 1931 Leyland-bodied Titan TD1, passes the old BCT office in Salford Bridge in June 1932, followed by one of Ribble's TD1s fitted with lowbridge Leyland bodywork.
Leyland Vehicles

Below: The only non-Leylands to enter the fleet between 1929 and 1943 were a pair of AEC Regents which arrived in 1939. These were the first Blackburn buses to be bodied by the local concern of East Lancashire Coachbuilders, which has supplied all new bodies to Blackburn since 1957. No 55 is seen in Blackburn bus station in postwar days.   *R. H. G. Simpson*

Right: Nineteen years separate these two Leyland Titans photographed in Accrington. Rawtenstall No 41 (XTJ 941D), a 1966 PD3/4 model with East Lancashire bodywork, gives way to Blackburn No 94, a Leyland-bodied PD1 dating from 1947, as it leaves the bus station on the Blackburn Express service.
T. W. Moore

Below right: Like its neighbour Accrington, Blackburn bought both Leylands and Guys after the war, the fleet in 1958/59 comprising 51 Leylands and 58 Guys. No 139, one of 20 Crossley-bodied Guy Arab IIIs delivered in 1949, overtakes East Lancashire-bodied Leyland Atlantean No 51, one of 10 new in 1968, in Ainsworth Street.
T. W. Moore

94
BLACKBURN-EXPRESS
100 Pipers:
the Scotch made for the rocks.
BBV
325
CAMERA CABIN
BACUP

139
CHERRY TREE
CBV
439
51
4 8 WILPSHIRE
KBV 51F

Borough of Blackburn Transport

Above: Though carrying Leyland lettering, No 179 (RTB 809M) is a Bristol RESL, one of three with East Lancashire bodies new to Darwen Corporation in 1973, the year before its absorption into the newly-formed Borough of Blackburn Transport fleet. When this photograph was taken in Church Street, Darwen, on 6 April 1984, these were the only saloons remaining in service. *John Robinson*

Right: After using a rather unattractive livery of dark green, red and white since 1974, Blackburn Transport took the popular step of reintroducing the 1929 livery of bright green and ivory, lined out in black in 1983. No 88, one of the 1972 batch of Leyland Atlanteans, is seen in Darwen's Circus on the same day, resplendent in its new colours. *John Robinson*

Below: The current fleet includes seven Dennis Dominators. No 4, one of five placed in service in 1981, received a special livery to mark the centenary of public transport in Blackburn and Darwen that year. It is depicted in Blackburn bus station on 4 May 1983 with Leyland Atlanteans dating from 1971 (No 80) and 1982 (No 17). *John Robinson*

Burnley, Colne & Nelson

Above: Burnley, Colne & Nelson took delivery of a pair of AEC Regal 4s in 1936 with Park Royal bodies of a very conservative design. No 149, photographed on 14 April 1952, remained in service until 1955.   *Roy Marshall*

Below: Burnley, Colne & Nelson bought several batches of Leyland Tigers after the war, and became the last UK operator to take delivery of new front-engined Tigers, with 14 PS2/14 models which were delivered in the 1953-55 period. Preceding these were six PS1/1s with Massey bodies, new in 1950, which included No 34, depicted in Nelson.   *M. A. Taylor*

Below: Leyland National No 143, one of a batch of 10 placed in service in 1974, leaves Burnley bus station for Rosegrove on 14 January 1982.   *John Robinson*

Bottom: Burnley & Pendle's current double-deck fleet is composed entirely of Bristol VRs 30 of the model being operated. The initial batch of 14, delivered in 1976, was bodied by East Lancashire and is typified by No 155, photographed calling at Burnley bus station on an evening working to Habergham on 1 February 1984.   *John Robinson*

Darwen

Above: Darwen No 21 (DTD 404), one of a batch of four Leyland Tiger TS8s with Burlingham bodies placed in service in 1938, is seen parked on the garage forecourt in postwar days. *Don Morris*

Left: Three Leyland Titan PD2/20s were added to the fleet in 1955, two bodied by Crossley and the third by East Lancashire. No 14, the first of those with Crossley bodywork, is depicted as it turns into Church Street, on leaving Darwen bus station. *R. H. G. Simpson*

Below left: Darwen operated a small number of Crossley DD42s after the war and, following the merger of AEC and Crossley, bought four AEC models with Crossley badges in 1957-58. These comprised a Crossley Regent and three Crossley Reliances, all bodied by East Lancashire. No 20, the final Reliance, is depicted in the town's small bus station. *R. H. G. Simpson*

Haslingden

Above: Well maintained prewar vehicles could be found in many municipal fleets. One of the finest examples was Haslingden's No 21 (CTJ 540), an all-Leyland Titan TD5 new in 1938, photographed outside the undertaking's small garage in John Street. Parked behind is Rawtenstall Corporation No 59 (738 NTD), an East Lancashire-bodied Leyland Tiger Cub new in 1960. *H. W. Peers*

Above right: Four Leyland Tigers with Burlingham 35-seat bodies were placed in service by Haslingden Corporation at the end of the 1940s. Depicted in this view is No 2, a PS1 model new in 1949. *Roy Marshall*

Right: Also numbered 2, but rather a different vehicle, was DTJ 960E, a 1967 Leyland Titan PD3/14 which was the last bus to enter the Haslingden fleet before its merger with neighbouring Rawtenstall in 1968. In common with all other new buses placed in service by the Corporation from 1954, East Lancashire bodywork was fitted. It is shown at Rawtenstall bus station on the Bacup-Rawtenstall-Haslingden-Accrington service which was operated jointly by the Corporations of the last three named towns. *R. H. G. Simpson*

Rawtenstall

Above: Rawtenstall took delivery of a solitary Guy Arab II in 1943. Originally fitted with a Massey body, it was photographed on 4 August 1953 carrying the East Lancashire body fitted in 1951. On rebodying, the radiator and bonnet were changed to the Arab III type, complete with the Red Indian's head, leaving little indication to the layman of its utility origin. In this form No 37 remained in service until 1964.   *Roy Marshall*

Left: Depicted in Rawtenstall before departing for Waterfoot, No 57 was the undertaking's first Leyland Tiger Cub. Carrying Weymann bodywork, it was built in July 1953 for use as a Leyland demonstrator, being placed in service by Rawtenstall in December 1954. Two further Tiger Cubs, with East Lancashire bodywork, joined the fleet in 1958 and 1960.   *Roy Marshall*

Top: Rawtenstall, and its successor Rossendale, standardised on Leyland Leopards with East Lancashire bodywork for single-deck deliveries between 1964 and 1973. No 62, one of six new in 1971, turns into Hall Carr Road, Rawtenstall, en route from Balladen to Britannia on 6 April 1984. *John Robinson*

Above: Seen in Bacup Road, Rawtenstall returning from a lunchtime run to Cowpe, No 50 was one of a pair of Bristol LHS models with East Lancashire 28-seat bodywork bought in 1982 to operate services over some of the less accessible roads in the borough. *John Robinson*

Preston

Above: Basking in the sunshine at Deepdale Road garage, Preston Corporation No 80 was an English Electric-bodied Leyland Tiger TS4 dating from 1933, its original body having been extensively modernised by the time this postwar view was taken. *Don Morris*

Below: Preston embarked on a unique programme of rebuilding Leyland-bodied PD2s as PD3s. Eight such vehicles, designated Leyland PD3/6, were constructed between 1959 and 1967. No 61, the penultimate conversion, dating from 1965, is seen at the garage. *Roy Marshall*

Above: The only non-Leylands ever bought by Preston were three Bristol LHSs with Duple Dominant 31-seat bodywork which were purchased in 1976 to operate new services over narrow estate roads. No 42, the only member of the batch fitted with coach seats, passes the Guild Hall on 9 April 1984 as it heads out to Grange Estate.   *John Robinson*

Below: Preston bought this Leyland Olympian coach with Eastern Coach Works 74-seat bodywork early in 1984. Numbered 3, it started its career by being loaned to Leyland Bus for use as a demonstrator. It is depicted leaving Warrington Central station operating a Sunday rail replacement service to Glazebrook whilst on loan to Warrington Transport in April 1984.   *John Robinson*

Lytham St Annes

Above: For some years the Lytham St Annes undertaking standardised on Leyland buses with the 'Gearless' torque converter transmission. This 1937 all-Leyland Lion LT7c, No 40 (BTC 624), photographed in St Annes in May of that year, proudly displays its 'Gearless Bus' emblem, which was less frequently seen on single-deckers, most recipients of this form of transmission being Leyland Titans. *Leyland Vehicles*

Left: Dating from 1943, Lytham St Annes No 22 was one of a pair of Daimler CWA6s fitted with Duple bodies to that concern's standard utility outline. Lytham's previous standardisation on Gearless Leylands could well have influenced the choice of Daimler chassis, since the fluid flywheel allowed similarly smooth restarts from rest to be accomplished. *W. J. Haynes*

Above: The current fleet contains a number of coaches, purchased as a result of the undertaking's increased committment to private hire operations. No 42, a Plaxton-bodied Leyland Leopard delivered in 1975, was the oldest coach owned when photographed leaving Aintree racecourse on Grand National day, 1983.
John Robinson

Below: Leyland Atlanteans have been standardised upon for double-deck requirements since 1970, all fitted with Northern Counties bodywork (though some are nominally by Willowbrook). No 95, dating from 1979, takes a party through Blackpool illuminations on 26 October 1983. The lettering on the side of the bus reads '1923 Blue Buses Diamond Jubilee 1983', whilst a sticker for '100 Years of Municipal Transport 1883 to 1983' is in place on the second upper-saloon window.
John Robinson

Blackpool

Left: Blackpool Corporation standardised upon Leyland Titans with fully-fronted centre-entrance bodywork for its double-deck fleet between 1936 and 1950. The initial 'streamlined' body was constructed by English Electric, but all subsequent ones were built in the town by Burlingham. Typifying the final development of this flamboyant style, which was unique to Blackpool, is No 216, one of the last batch of 100, which were placed in service in 1949-50. Based on PD2/5 chassis, these buses survived until the late 1960s. *Robert F. Mack*

Below: Leyland Titans continued to be specified by Blackpool as late as 1968, all but the first five being bodied by Metro-Cammell. Those delivered up to 1964 continued the tradition of having full-width cabs, albeit on an otherwise standard rear-entrance body, but subsequent batches reverted to the half-cab layout. Representative of the latter is No 503, a PD3A/1 model placed in service in 1967, which was one of the few surviving Titans in the fleet when photographed at Talbot Road bus station operating an evening journey to Fleetwood on 26 October 1983. *John Robinson*

Above: Between 1969 and 1975 55 AEC Swifts with Marshall 47-seat dual-doorway bodywork entered the fleet. No 570, seen at Rigby Road garage on 17 August 1978, was one of the 1974 batch.   *John Robinson*

Below: Marshall bodywork was also specified for four Dennis Lancets which were added to the fleet in 1982. No 599, the last of the batch, is pursued by No 325 (URN 325V), one of the undertaking's large fleet of East Lancashire-bodied Leyland Atlanteans, as it heads along Talbot Road en route to Poulton in July 1983.
T. W. Moore

LANCASTER AND MORECAMBE BAY

Lancaster

Above: Lancaster City Transport was a keen Daimler operator in prewar days. No 383, a 1940 COG5 model with attractive Willowbrook bodywork, stands in Lancaster bus station wearing the postwar livery. Behind is Ribble Leyland Titan TD4 No 1602 (RN 7869), fitted with a postwar Burlingham body, operating to Penrhyn Road on a service run jointly with LCT. *Roy Marshall*

Above left: A number of utility Guy Arabs were supplied to Lancaster, some of which were fitted with rare Pickering bodywork. One such vehicle was No 69, an Arab I model, which was originally numbered 43 when delivered in 1943. This concern's wartime double-deck body was unusual in having chromium-plated frames to the windscreen and opening windows, rare features at that time, which can be seen in this view at Lancaster bus station on 30 May 1952. Parked behind is one of Lancaster's Crossley DD42s. *Roy Marshall*

Left: Photographed at Skerton Bridge en route for Beaumont, No 202 was one of three Leyland Titan PD2/37s with East Lancashire forward-entrance bodies placed in service in 1963. All three passed to the newly-formed Lancaster City Council Passenger Transport Department in 1974, and were converted to open-toppers in 1976 (No 201) and 1977 (Nos 202 and 203), continuing in service until 1980. *Roy Marshall*

Morecambe & Heysham

Right: AEC Regents first appeared in the Morecambe & Heysham fleet in 1932 and, apart from five Leyland Titans delivered in the early 1960s, all buses purchased up to 1970 were of AEC manufacture. Regent III No 77, photographed at the Battery on 1 August 1973, was one of six with Weymann bodywork placed in service in 1951. *John Robinson*

Below: Also at the Battery, No 91 was one of the five Leyland Titans in the fleet, all fitted with Massey 64-seat forward-entrance bodywork. The first three, new in 1960, were exposed radiator PD2/37 models, whilst the final pair, delivered two years later, were fitted with the fibreglass 'St Helens' bonnet assembly, and designated PD2A/27. *Roy Marshall*

Above: Ten AEC Swifts were bought between 1967 and 1970, enabling the undertaking to introduce one man operation. No 10, the last of these, and one of three with Northern Counties bodywork, is seen at Heysham bus station on 9 June 1973. *John Robinson*

BATTERY
77
MTE639

Lancaster City Council

Above right: The Lancaster City Transport and Morecambe & Heysham Corporation fleets were amalgamated in April 1974 to form the Lancaster City Council Passenger Transport Department. All new buses placed in service since that date have been of Leyland manufacture, the first being 12 Leyland Leopards with Alexander bodywork which entered the fleet in 1976, with a further 14 similar vehicles following in 1977. No 303, one of the first intake, crosses Skerton Bridge, Lancaster, on 20 May 1978 operating service U3 from Morecambe to Lancaster University.   *John Robinson*

Right: 33ft long Leyland Atlanteans with East Lancashire bodywork have been standardised upon for double-deck deliveries. Nos 205 and 206, both dating from 1981, are seen parked on the M66 near Manchester during the Papal visit to nearby Heaton Park on 31 May 1982. Standing between is Alexander-bodied Leyland Leopard coach No 19, some four years older.   *John Robinson*

Below: Photographed heading along Morecambe's promenade for Heysham Village on 17 August 1976 during its first season as an open-topper, No 201 provides an interesting comparison with the much earlier view of sister vehicle No 202 operating with Lancaster City Transport.   *John Robinson*

Cheshire and North Wales

Chester

Right: Between 1953 and 1969 Chester Corporation standardised on Guy Arabs for its double-deck requirements, the double-deck fleet in 1970 being composed exclusively of this model, until the first Daimler Fleetlines arrived at the end of that year. Virtually all the Guys were fitted with Massey bodywork and No 15, one of eight Mark IVs placed in service in 1955, typifies this bodybuilder's attractive design of the period as it heads along Eastgate Street, with Chester's celebrated clock tower dominating the skyline.
T. W. Moore

Below: Chester acquired two Willowbrook-bodied AEC Reliances from SELNEC PTE in 1973, both of which had been taken over from North Western, to whom they were new in 1961. No 64, numerically the first, but actually the second to enter service, doing so in February 1974, is seen running empty along Union Street on 25 July 1974. Both vehicles had a brief career with Chester, being withdrawn at the end of 1976.
John Robinson

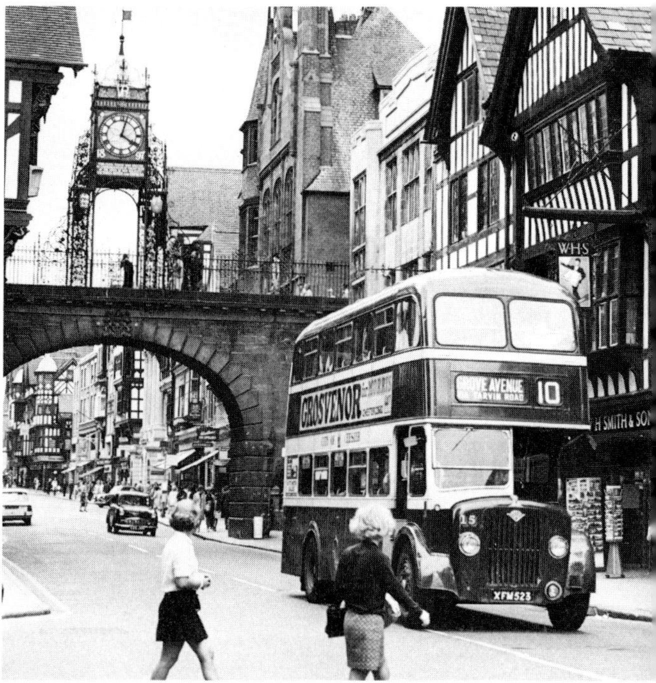

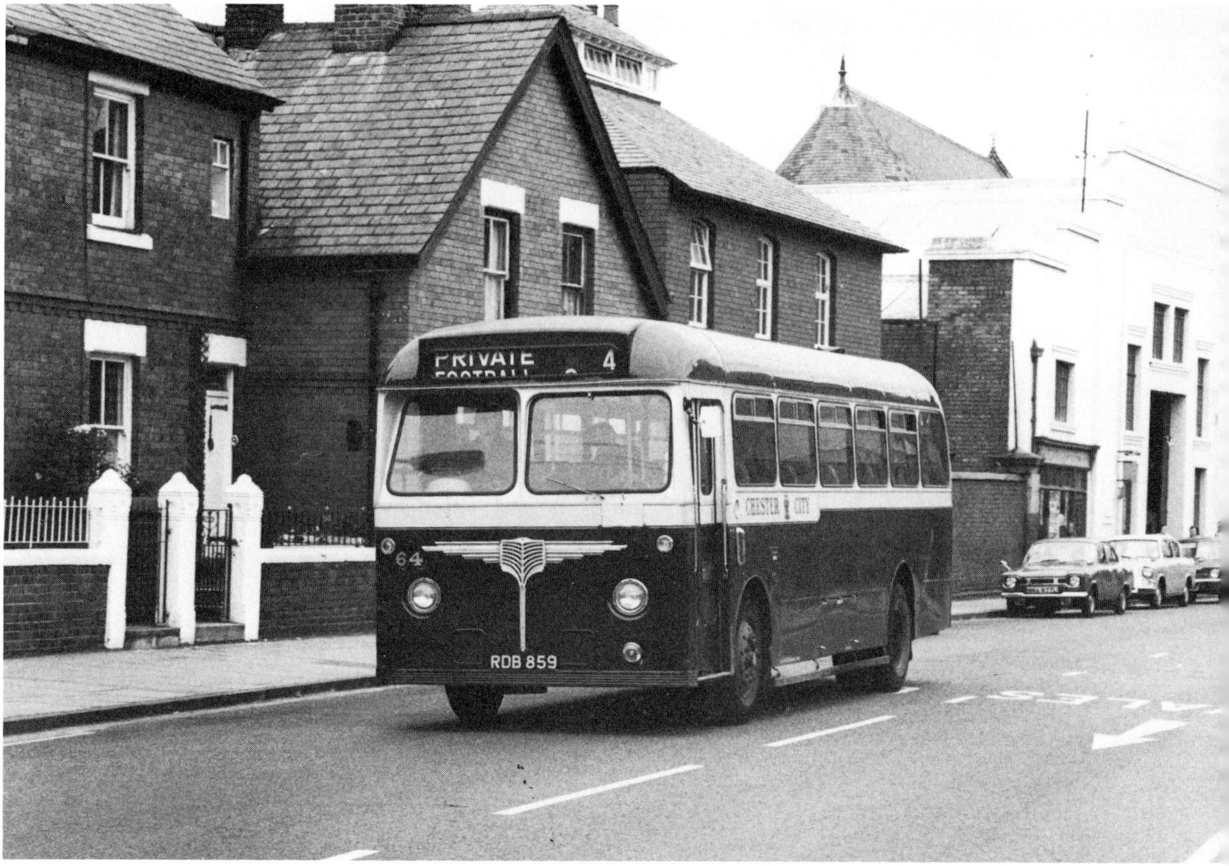

Right: After the production of Guy Arabs ceased in 1969 Chester turned to Daimler Fleetlines, and continued to purchase the model until 1980, by which time 30, all with Northern Counties bodywork, were in service. No 55, the first of the 1972 intake, is seen turning into Eastgate Street on 23 February 1983. *John Robinson*

Below: 1976 deliveries comprised nine Leyland Leopards, delivered in two batches, which entered service in January and December. The first three (Nos 69-71) were bodied by Northern Counties, Chester's usual bodybuilder, but the second batch (Nos 75-80) received Duple Dominant 47-seat bus bodywork, becoming the first Duple single-deck bodies to enter the fleet since 1934. No 78 (TMB 878R) crosses the Old Dee Bridge on its way into the city centre on 21 May 1983, passing a Dennis Dominator heading in the opposite direction. *John Robinson*

Colwyn Bay

Above: Having purchased nothing other than Guys since it commenced operations in 1925, Colwyn Bay switched to Bedfords in 1954. No 4, a J2LZ2 model with Spurling 21-seat bodywork, was one of two new in 1960, and is seen at the Pier before setting off on the Promenade service.   *Robert F. Mack*

Below: A later Bedford, photographed heading along the promenade, was DTM 870D, one of a pair of J2SZ10 models with Plaxton 20-seat bodywork that were obtained second-hand from Bletchley Self Drive in 1968. Both continued in service with Colwyn Bay until 1975. *Roy Marshall*

Llandudno

Top: Llandudno Urban District Council Transport Department favoured small-capacity Guys for many years. CCC 596, one of a pair of Guy Otters with Roe 25-seat bodywork new in 1954, is depicted at the tours stand on the Promenade. *Roy Marshall*

Above: Seen ascending the Great Orme on the service from Llandudno town centre to St Tudno's Church, KCC 783P was one of two Bedford SB5s with Willowbrook bodywork placed in service by Llandudno UDC's successor, Aberconwy Borough Council, in 1976. Their seating capacity of 41 makes them the largest vehicles ever owned by the undertaking. *Robert F. Mack*

Warrington

Left: Warrington and neighbouring St Helens were the only municipal operators in the North Western Traffic Area to buy postwar Bristol K models. Twenty-nine K6Gs were placed in service by Warrington Corporation between 1947 and 1950, all but two carrying bodywork by Bruce Coach Works of Cardiff. No 69, one of the last batch, is seen on layover at Bank Quay station before setting off for Appleton Thorn on the service operated jointly with Naylors Motor Services of Stockton Heath. *Robert F. Mack*

Below: Warrington Corporation was famous for its fleet of Foden double-deckers, building up a fleet of 15 PVD6s between 1948 and 1956, out of a total production of only 61. No 104 (MED 170), standing in Bridge Street, was one of three with Crossley bodies delivered in 1954-55. *Roy Marshall*

Above: Single-deck requirements were fulfilled by Bristol REs between 1968 and 1975. No 68, dating from 1975, turns into Golborne Street on 22 August 1981, operating as a two-man bus, followed by Leyland Atlantean No 77 in Warrington Festival livery. Both carry East Lancashire bodies. *John Robinson*

Below: Another view of No 77, picking up school children in August 1981. This was one of the first Leyland Atlanteans to enter the Warrington fleet, doing so in May 1977 when it carried special lettering to commemorate the Queen's Silver Jubilee; the Warrington Festival livery shown was applied in 1980. *John Robinson*

Widnes

Right: Widnes embarked on a programme of rebodying some of its utility Daimler CWA6s in the mid 1950s, producing buses like No 53, which had a 1955 East Lancashire body on a 1943 chassis. The Widnes idiosyncracy of specifying one fixed and one opening window at the front can be seen. *Don Morris*

Below: Four ex-London Transport Weymann-bodied AEC Regent IIs, acquired via North (dealer), Leeds, were placed in service in August 1955. No 22, standing in St Pauls Road, was amongst the last 20 buses added to LT's famous STL-class, having been delivered as STL2682 in February 1946. All four were withdrawn between 1960-62, the vehicle shown subsequently becoming a mobile office with Widnes Corporation Building Department. *Don Morris*

Below: The first postwar single-deckers in the fleet were a pair of all-Leyland Royal Tiger PSU1/13s bought in 1952 to replace the two remaining Leyland Lions, dating from 1935. No 18, photographed passing the Swan Hotel at Winwick (to the north of Warrington) on a private hire, remained in service until 1971.
M. A. Taylor

Bottom: Very unusual additions to the Halton fleet in 1975 were two Leyland Leopards with East Lancashire 49-seat coach bodywork. The first, No 8, is seen in Chester after working in on a private hire on 7 July 1976. The only other operator with this type of body was Hyndburn, which bought one on a Seddon Pennine RU chassis in 1974. Halton's two coaches were rebodied with East Lancashire bus bodies in 1983, whilst the Hyndburn coach was withdrawn the same year.
John Robinson

LUNCHEONS & TEAS
COMMERCIAL
SPECIAL
18
NTD 253

SPECIAL
HALTON
JFV 294N
LEYLAND

SELNEC PTE – CONSTITUENT FLEETS

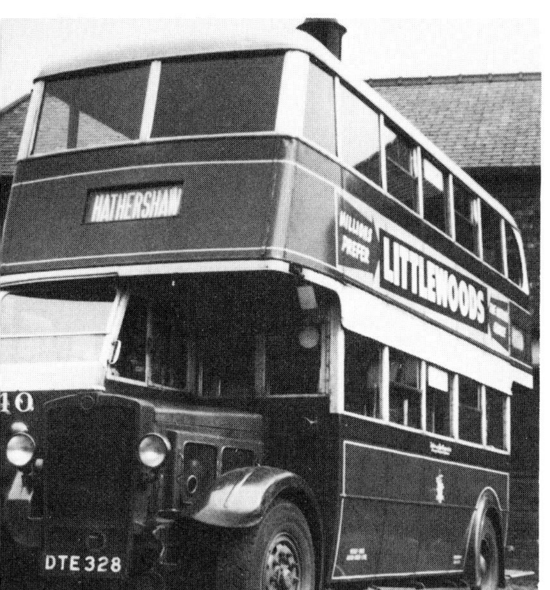

Ashton-under-Lyne

Left: Ashton No 40, a Crossley-bodied Crossley Mancunian new in 1939, wearing the red, white and blue livery which gave way to the more familiar peacock blue and cream after 1954. *Don Morris*

Below: Ashton's Nos 61-64 were Sunbeam W trolleybuses with Park Royal bodies placed in service in 1944. All four were rebodied in the 1950s, Nos 61 and 62 by Roe in 1958 and Nos 63 and 64 by Bond, the Wythenshawe concern, in 1955 and 1954 respectively. No 64, photographed in Portland Street, Manchester, remained in service until 1963, and was the first bus to wear the peacock blue and cream livery, with the addition of a scarlet band above the lower saloon windows, which was omitted on subsequent repaints. Behind are two Burlingham-bodied BUT 9612Ts of Manchester Corporation which, along with Ashton, was the only operator of this model, built at the Crossley works. *R. H. G. Simpson*

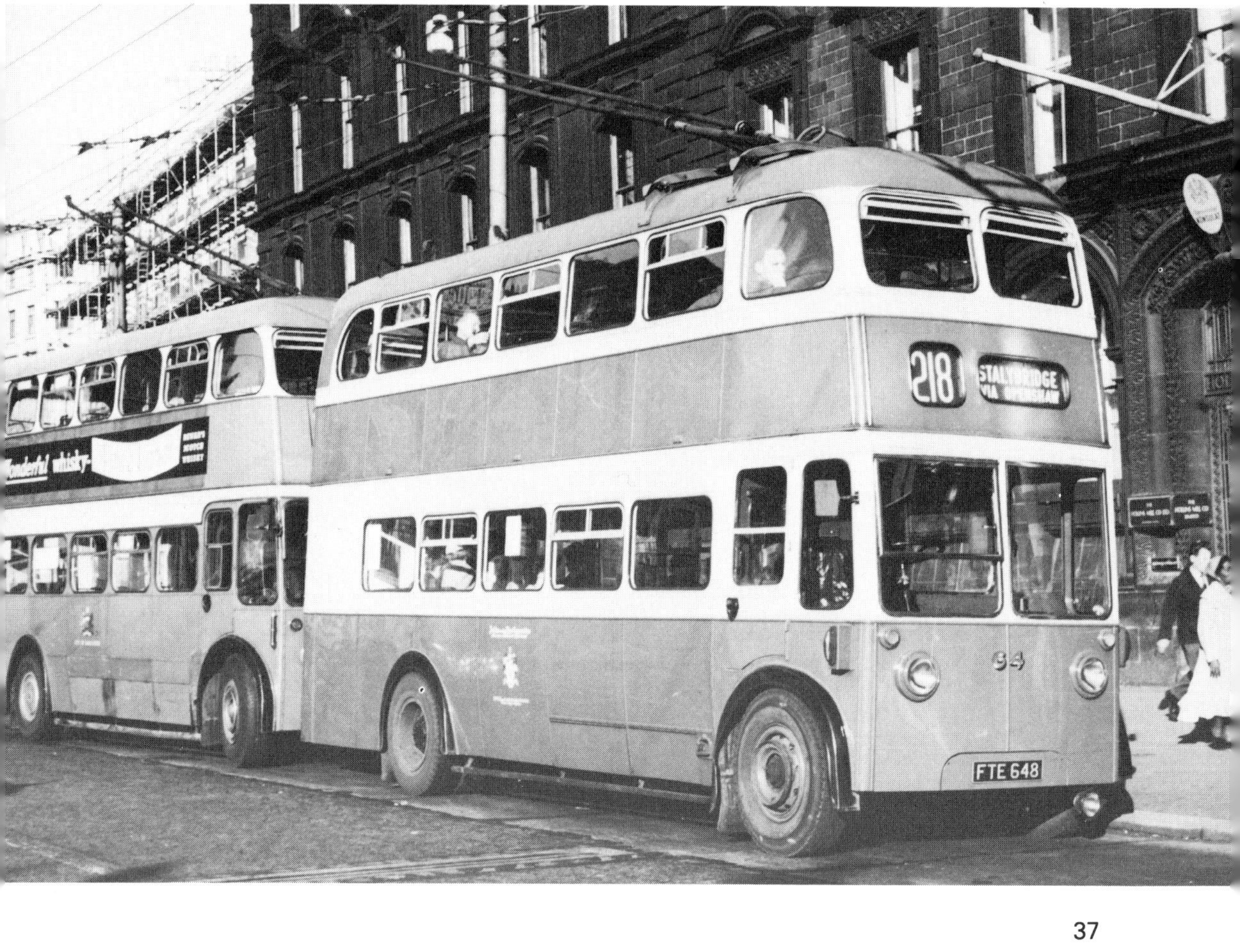

Above: Bond also bodied four Guy Arab IVs for Ashton in 1956. The finished buses were of very pleasing appearance, as this view of No 38 parked in Sackville Street, outside Ashton railway station, shows.
Roy Marshall

Right: Between 1960 and 1964 24 of these Roe-bodied Leyland Titan PD2/40s entered the fleet, in four batches. No 20, from the first batch, leaves Manchester Piccadilly for Stalybridge.   *T. W. Moore*

Bolton

Above: Bolton took delivery of this Metro-Cammell-bodied AEC Q in 1933. The ultra-modern vehicle failed to impress the Corporation, however, and no repeat orders were placed; in fact only 23 double-deck Qs were built. The tramway-style lifeguard beneath the front overhang was fitted to allay fears about the alleged dangers of vehicles with a long front overhang, although in practice they were not found to be necessary, and most Qs, including this one, had them removed in due course. *Real Photographs*

Right: Bolton Corporation was the third largest Crossley operator after Manchester and Birmingham. Seventy-five DD42/3 models were placed in service in 1946-47 before the purchase of Leylands was resumed. Their arrival expedited the tramway replacement programme, which was completed in 1947. Bolton's last Crossley double-decker, No 320, stands in Spinning Jenny Street bus station, Leigh, before departing for Horwich. This was one of only eight to be fitted with Crossley's own distinctive bodywork, the remaining 67 being bodied by Cravens. *Don Morris*

Below: Bolton was another Lancashire undertaking to specify Bond bodywork in 1956, for one Leyland Royal Tiger and nine Leyland Titan PD2/13s. Two of the Titans, Nos 71 and 74, are seen shortly after entering service. *M. A. Taylor*

Bottom: Thirty-six Daimler CVG6s entered the fleet between 1957 and 1960, 15 of them being the 30ft model. East Lancashire-bodied No 149, from the last batch of eight, is seen in Moor Lane bus station, wearing the brighter livery introduced in 1962. *Roy Marshall*

Bury

Left: Bury Corporation was one of the few undertakings to operate Leyland Titanics. No 52 (EN 6051), a TT2 model, fitted with centre-entrance English Electric bodywork, was one of five placed in service in 1934. It is seen in The Rock loading for Jericho in July 1936. *Leyland Vehicles*

Below: Another unusual Bury bus was No 101, the solitary Roe-bodied Guy Wulfrunian, which was new in 1960, and only lasted three years before being sold to a Welsh independent. In this view in Broad Street it is operating westbound on the cross-town Jericho-Tottington service, whilst in the distance No 205 (GEN 205), one of the 1958 Weymann-bodied Leyland Titan PD3/6s works the eastbound leg. Between them is Rochdale No 319 (TDK 319), one of the last four AEC Regent Vs delivered to the Corporation, also dating from 1958. *Roy Marshall*

Above: Photographed in Manchester Road, No 88 was one of a pair of Alexander-bodied AEC Reliances new in 1964. The same concern also bodied 15 Daimler Fleetlines for the Corporation that year, but virtually all subsequent orders for bodywork went to East Lancashire, until the undertaking was absorbed by SELNEC in November 1969. *Roy Marshall*

Below: Amongst the East Lancashire-bodied buses in the fleet were nine Daimler Fleetline saloons; three were placed in service in 1967, followed by a further six in 1969. From the first batch, 90 is seen on the Darn Hill estate at Heywood. *John Robinson collection*

Leigh

Top: Because of the restricted clearance in Leigh Corporation's garage, all double-deckers were of lowbridge, and later lowheight, configuration. No 47 (TJ 3451), a Massey-bodied Leyland Titan TD3, was one of a pair delivered in 1933, and is seen on a rather gloomy day in October 1934. *Leyland Vehicles*

Above: Leyland's domination of the Leigh fleet was weakened in 1948, when the undertaking's first AECs arrived. No 26, photographed in the town's small bus station on 6 April 1963, was one of 12 Regent III 9612Es with Roberts bodywork placed in service in 1948-49, a further six Roberts bodies being mounted on Leyland Titan PD2/1 chassis at about the same time. *Roy Marshall*

Above: Six Dennis Lolines were operated by Leigh, being delivered in pairs in 1958, 1959 and 1961. The first four were Mk Is, whilst the 1961 intake was of Mk IIIs. All were fitted with East Lancashire 72-seat rear-entrance bodies, Leigh being the only operator to specify rear-entrance bodywork on Mk III chassis, which was designed to accommodate forward-entrance bodywork. No 61, one of the first pair, is depicted at Spinning Jenny Street bus station, Leigh, before departing for Bolton. *R. H. G. Simpson*

Right: Leigh No 1 (187 LTB), the first of a pair of East Lancashire-bodied Leyland Tiger Cubs new in 1960, picks up passengers in St Helens Road, Pennington, on its way into the town centre on a quiet Sunday morning in May 1965. *Roy Marshall*

Manchester

Above: For many years the mainstays of Manchester's single-deck fleet were 40 Leyland Tiger TS8s which were placed in service during the winter of 1937-38. Their 32-seat rear-entrance bodies were completed by Crossley on Metro-Cammell frames to the Corporation's then standard 'streamline' design. No 67 (DXJ 303), parked at Hyde Road works, displays the streamlined livery, which fell out of favour after the war. *W. J. Haynes*

Below: Manchester was by far the largest operator of trolleybuses in the North Western Traffic Area, introducing them in March 1938. No 1087, pictured at Rochdale Road trolleybus depot, was the last of a batch of 26 Leyland TTB4s new that year. The double-deck version of the Metro-Cammell/Crossley streamlined body is carried. This particular vehicle was withdrawn at the end of 1955. *Real Photographs: B1252*

Above: Manchester operated the largest fleet of Crossleys in the country. Typical of the DD42s was No 2953, a DD42/3 new in 1946 with Manchester-style Crossley bodywork. It contrasts markedly with the North Western utility Guy Arab II, No 24 (BJA 109), only one year older, which is loading for Northwich in this view at Piccadilly bus station, Manchester, on 10 September 1949. Fitted with Roe bodywork here, it was rebodied by Willowbrook the following year, remaining in service until 1963. It is of interest to note that North Western indulged in strict accuracy, referring to this location as 'Manchester Parker Street', whereas Manchester Corporation buses displayed the more up-market 'Piccadilly'. *Alan Cooper*

Below: Vast quantities of new buses entered the fleet in the early postwar years. No 3150 (JNA 451), seen passing the Town Hall on 9 September 1949, was one of 100 Leyland Titan PD1/3s new that year with Metro-Cammell bodywork to Manchester specification. Manchester was the first major city bus undertaking to commit itself to 100% adoption of the newly-permitted 8ft width in place of the previous 7ft 6in for all new buses ordered from 1946; hence the choice of the PD1/3 model of this width, which was also specified by Oldham Corporation and Ribble, but was virtually unknown elsewhere. *Alan Cooper*

Above: Northern Counties bodied 30 Leyland Titan PD2/12s for Manchester in 1953-54, one of which is seen in Piccadilly bus station operating to Gatley. The wide upper-deck centre pillar housed the air exchanger system, introduced by Northern Counties in 1949, which kept the upper-deck clear of tobacco smoke. Perforated panels were fitted along the ceiling, the stale air being drawn through the perforations by air induction from the engine. *M. A. Taylor*

Above left: Manchester's first Metro-Cammell Orion bodies were fitted to 10 Daimler CVG6s which entered service in 1955. The initial vehicle of the batch, No 4480 (NNB 290), is seen on a special duty when new. *John Robinson collection*

Left: Manchester Corporation was the first operator to place a Leyland Panther Cub in service, a total of 20 being added to the fleet in 1964-65, followed by 30 of the larger-engined Panther model in 1967. Panther Cub No 76, fitted with Park Royal dual-doorway bodywork, is seen on hire to Southport Corporation when new. *R. H. G. Simpson*

Overleaf: In 1968 Manchester Corporation received its first 96 purpose-built OMO double-deckers, divided equally between Leyland Atlantean and Daimler Fleetline chassis. Their Park Royal bodies were bravely painted in a mainly white livery, with red as the secondary colour. Christened 'Mancunians', Fleetline No 2021 heads along Market Street in November 1969, in a direction since rendered impossible by the city's one-way system. *T. W. Moore*

Oldham

Above: Like Manchester, Oldham Corporation was enthusiastic about adopting the newly-permitted 8ft width, taking delivery of 50 Leyland Titan PD1/3s with Roe bodies in 1947-48. No 253 stands in Smith Street, Rochdale, before setting off for Manchester. *Don Morris*

Below: Oldham took delivery of a batch of 10 Crossley SD42/3s in 1948, which were joined by four SD42/7 models two years later, both batches being fitted with 32-seat Roe bodywork. No 299, one of the 1948 intake, is seen in Oldham town centre before setting off for Mossley. *Roy Marshall*

Right: An order for 25 Daimler CVD6s was placed in the late 1940s, the body contract being split between Roe and Crossley. The 10 Roe-bodied vehicles arrived at the end of 1948, whilst the others appeared the following year. No 336 (EBU 936), the last of those bodied by Crossley, is seen shortly after entering service.
Roy Marshall

Below: 'Tin-front' Leyland Titans were introduced to Oldham Corporation in 1954 when a batch of 15 PD2/20s arrived, five bodied by Metro-Cammell, and the remainder by Oldham's more usual bodybuilder, Roe. No 375, one of the Metro-Cammell-bodied vehicles, is seen on the Ashton-Oldham-Rochdale service.
M. A. Taylor

Ramsbottom

Above left: Standing outside the small garage in Stubbins Lane, Ramsbottom No 8 was one of a pair of Roe-bodied Leyland Tiger TS7s delivered in 1937. Visible in the background is all-Leyland Titan PD2/1 No 20 (HTF 815), one of a batch of six new in 1947, which were the first double-deckers in the fleet. *Don Morris*

Left: Another Roe-bodied saloon in the Ramsbottom fleet, No 28 was one of three Leyland Royal Tigers new in 1950. All were sold to neighbouring corporations in the early 1960s, No 26 going to Rawtenstall and Nos 27 and 28 to Haslingden. *M. A. Taylor*

Below: Ramsbottom had the distinction of being the recipient of the last Leyland Titan built, which was a PD3/14 model with East Lancashire 73-seat forward-entrance bodywork. Although it was finished in full Ramsbottom livery, it did not enter service with the council, being licensed by the newly-formed SELNEC PTE in November 1969. Numbered 11 by Ramsbottom, it is seen climbing Rochdale Road, Edenfield when new, with snow-covered Scout Moor in the distance. *Leyland Vehicles*

Rochdale

Above: After the war Rochdale purchased AECs and, to a lesser extent, Daimlers, exclusively, thus becoming the only municipal undertaking in Lancashire not to operate Leyland Titan PDs. However, a number of TDs were delivered prewar; No 128 (BDK 355), photographed passing Rochdale's inspiring Town Hall in February 1938, was one of a pair of Weymann-bodied TD4cs placed in service in 1936.   *Leyland Vehicles*

Left: Rochdale No 23 (EDK 923), a 1945 Daimler CWD6 with Massey body of that concern's immediate post-utility type, stands in Cannon Street, Manchester before setting off for home on 3 October 1948.
Roy Marshall

Above right: Two batches of AEC Regal IVs were placed in service in the early 1950s. Depicted at Bamford, No 4 was one of the first batch of seven fitted with East Lancashire bodies which were new in 1951.
Robert F. Mack

Right: Rochdale's first rear-engined buses were five Daimler Fleetlines which arrived in 1964. Weymann bodies of standard outline were fitted, although the lower-deck side windows were located about 6in higher than usual, as can be seen on this view of No 325 swinging into The Esplanade.   *Roy Marshall*

BAMFORD
5
BURY ROAD
ROCHDALE CORPORATION
4

ROCHDALE
HEYWOOD
HEAP BRIDGE
THE ROCK
325
6325 DK

Salford

Above : Salford reconditioned 10 prewar Leyland TD chassis in 1948-49 and had them fitted with new Burlingham bodies. Photographed in Chapel Street, just after leaving its Greengate terminus, No 106 was a 1935 TD4 which was originally bodied by Metro-Cammell and carried fleetnumber 31.   *Robert F. Mack*

Below: Salford No 451, a Daimler CVG6 with Burlingham 22-seat bodywork, was the City Transport Committee's coach from 1950 to 1962, although it saw very little use. It is seen at Frederick Road garage on 22 July 1951, on the occasion of an Omnibus Society visit. Parked alongside are No 450 (CRJ 450), a 1950 Daimler CVG6/Burlingham; No 108 (RJ 3008), a 1934 Leyland TD3/Burlingham (1949 body); No 261 (BRJ 915), a 1947 Crossley DD42/3/Metro-Cammell; and a 1947 AEC Regent/Metro-Cammell.   *Roy Marshall*

Above: Photographed in Cook Street, Leigh after arriving from Manchester, No 500 was one of 195 Daimler CVG6s with Metro-Cammell bodywork to Salford specification delivered between 1950 and 1952. These were the undertaking's first 8ft wide buses, and until the majority of the fleet were of this width they carried a small red dome on the bottom of the front upper-saloon window pillar to remind the bus wash operator of their extra width.   *Don Morris*

Above right: Ten Weymann-bodied AEC Reliances were placed in service in 1962; the first (No 101) had Fanfare 26-seat coach bodywork, whilst the other nine had 45-seat bus bodies. No 104 is seen leaving Victoria bus station for Peel Green.   *Roy Marshall*

Right: Salford bought 103 of these Metro-Cammell-bodied Leyland Titan PD2/40s between 1963 and 1967. No 174, one of the first batch, crosses Trafford Road swing bridge en route from Swinton Park to Stretford.   *T. W. Moore*

Stalybridge, Hyde, Mossley & Dukinfield Transport Board

Below: Stalybridge, Hyde, Mossley & Dukinfield Transport Board was a keen supporter of Thornycroft, all buses entering service between 1925 and 1936 being of this make. No 134 (LG 4612), photographed at Lower Mosley Street bus station, Manchester, was one of 24 Thornycroft LCs with Northern Counties bodywork which entered the fleet between December 1929 and May 1930. *W. J. Haynes*

Bottom: When Thornycroft ceased production of buses, Daimler was adopted as the new standard. No 52 (LMA 752), seen in Ashton-under-Lyne en route to Stockport, was one of 10 CVD6s delivered in 1949. SHMD's fleet was almost exclusively bodied by Northern Counties, but these buses broke with tradition by having East Lancashire bodies. All subsequent orders, however, reverted to Northern Counties. *Don Morris*

Above: A solitary Daimler Freeline was placed in service in 1953, and is shown in Ashton-under-Lyne before setting off for Uppermill. The Northern Counties central-entrance 'standee' bodywork was similar in appearance to ones supplied to Manchester Corporation on Leyland Royal Tiger chassis and Lancashire United Transport on Atkinson Alpha chassis.   *Roy Marshall*

Below: A sprinkling of Leyland Titans infiltrated the fleet between 1958 and 1962. No 90, photographed at Lower Mosley Street on hire to North Western, was one of 10 PD2/40s with Northern Counties rear-entrance bodies which entered service in 1958/59.   *M. A. Taylor*

Stockport

Above: Photographed in Parrs Wood on driver training duties in postwar days, Stockport No 189 (JA 7589) was one of a batch of 10 Leyland Tiger TS7s with attractive English Electric half-canopy, centre-entrance bodywork delivered in 1936.   *Robert F. Mack*

Below: Stockport Corporation was the recipient of the last two Crossley Mancunians built, placing them in service in 1941, with Manchester-style Crossley bodies on Metro-Cammell frames. No 205, seen in Mersey Square on 4 April 1953, remained in service until 1958. Behind is No 177 (JA 7577), an all-Leyland Titan TD4c dating from 1936.   *Roy Marshall*

Right: A number of Massey-bodied Guy Arab II utilities were delivered in 1943-45. No 210 (JA 7610), passing Mersey Square depot in more or less original condition, was one of the 1943 vehicles.   *Roy Marshall*

Below right: Stockport, like Ramsbottom, was a late recipient of the Leyland Titan, a total of 27 PD3/14s with East Lancashire bodies entering service in 1968-69. No 91 runs into Manchester Piccadilly bus station, followed by Titans from the Salford and Manchester fleets. *T. W. Moore*

STOCKPORT
STEPPING HILL
810

GOOD YEAR
TYRES
MANCHESTER
PICCADILLY
91
MJA 891G

Wigan

Above: Leyland buses first appeared in the Wigan Corporation fleet in 1927 and, apart from Bristol and Guy utilities, all buses purchased from 1929 were of this make. No 105 (JP 3534), photographed outside the undertaking's offices in Market Place on 4 August 1953, was one of three Leyland Lion LT9s with locally-built Northern Counties bodies which entered service in 1938. *Roy Marshall*

Below: Wigan No 128 (JP 5135) was one of three Bristol K6As allocated to the undertaking by the Ministry of War Transport and received early in 1945. Fitted with Strachans lowbridge bodywork, the number of opening windows, restricted on most utilities to two on each side (as on the bus behind), had been increased by the time this photograph was taken on 9 July 1949.
Roy Marshall

Right: The last Leyland-bodied buses to enter the Wigan fleet were 12 Titan PD2/12 models new in 1953. No 63, seen in Millgate, illustrates the ultimate development of Leyland's classic double-deck body, production of which ceased the following year. Heading in the opposite direction is No 52 (KEK 745), a 1964 Titan PD2A/27 bodied by Northern Counties.   *Robert F. Mack*

Below right: Eight Leyland Titan PD2A/27s were placed in service in 1963, equal numbers being bodied by Massey and Northern Counties. No 133, bodied by the latter concern, passes through Blackrod on the Horwich-Wigan service on 28 May 1974, nearly two months after the takeover by Greater Manchester Transport, but bearing no evidence of its new owner.
John Robinson

22
MARSH GREEN
WIGAN CORPORATION
63
63
AEK 505
EXCHANGE YOU
TIMBERL
CAR & COMMERCIAL VEHICLE
USED CAR SPECIA

6
WIGAN
LEYLAND
JJP 509

SELNEC and Greater Manchester Transport

Above: On its formation SELNEC inherited a number of orders placed by constituent undertakings. One such order, placed by Bolton Corporation, was for 15 East Lancashire-bodied Leyland Atlantean PDR2s, which were delivered in 1971-72, incorporating SELNEC interiors and destination indicators. No 6807 is seen turning into Higher Swan Lane, Bolton on 13 October 1973, operating the Swan Lane/Great Lever circular. *John Robinson*

Left: North Western had 25 Bristol VRs on order at the time of its acquisition, which were delivered direct to SELNEC in 1973. Their Eastern Coach Works bodies incorporated SELNEC destination indicators, although the offside aperture was originally blocked off. No 411 is seen heading along Buxton Road, Stockport, on 10 March 1973, en route from Hazel Grove to Manchester. *John Robinson*

Above : The majority of double-deckers which SELNEC took over from North Western were Alexander-bodied Daimler Fleetlines. No 103, a 1964 example, is seen turning into Stamford New Road, Altrincham from Kingsway on 23 August 1974. *John Robinson*

Below: SELNEC, and its successor Greater Manchester Transport, placed 43 Seddon-bodied Seddon IV midibuses in service between 1972-75. The last 28 were of the 'Cityline' type, with Allison automatic gearboxes and a special livery – top half orange, lower half white – for use on the Manchester and Bolton Centreline services. Bolton's Centreline service finished in 1975, but the one in Manchester, which links Piccadilly and Victoria railway stations, thrives. Operating an evening journey on 13 March 1984 is No 1724, one of the Queens Road allocation. *John Robinson*

Above: Most of the coaches taken over with the Lancashire United Transport fleet in April 1981 were Plaxton Supreme-bodied Leyland Leopards. Four of the oldest ones, dating from 1977, were subsequently transferred to Northenden garage to operate the Airport Express 200 service, for which they received a special orange, white, blue and brown livery. These vehicles are also used on other services, as exemplified by No 38 leaving Piccadilly bus station for Wythenshawe on 20 June 1984. *John Robinson*

Below: An assorted fleet of Leyland Nationals was built up between 1972 and 1979. No 187, an 11.3m single-doorway model dating from 1979, was one of the last 20 to enter the fleet new, and is seen passing Bickershaw Colliery on its way back into Leigh from Crankwood on 21 April 1983. *John Robinson*

Right: Greater Manchester Transport's first production standard double-deckers were placed in service in 1972, the model continuing to be specified until 1984, by which time 1,725 had been built. Most standards were Northern Counties-bodied Leyland Atlanteans although Daimler Fleetlines and, later, Leyland Fleetlines were also specified, whilst 360 bodies were constructed by Park Royal. No 8585, a Leyland Atlantean/Northern Counties combination, typifies the light alloy standard body, introduced in 1981, as it passes Princess Road garage, Moss Side on 26 March 1983, wearing Bus & Coach Council livery. *John Robinson*

Below right: Nearly 200 Metro-Cammell-bodied MCW Metrobuses were placed in service between 1979 and 1983. Typical of these is No 5175, depicted crossing Trafford Road swing bridge on a rush-hour working of service 71 on 5 March 1984. *John Robinson*

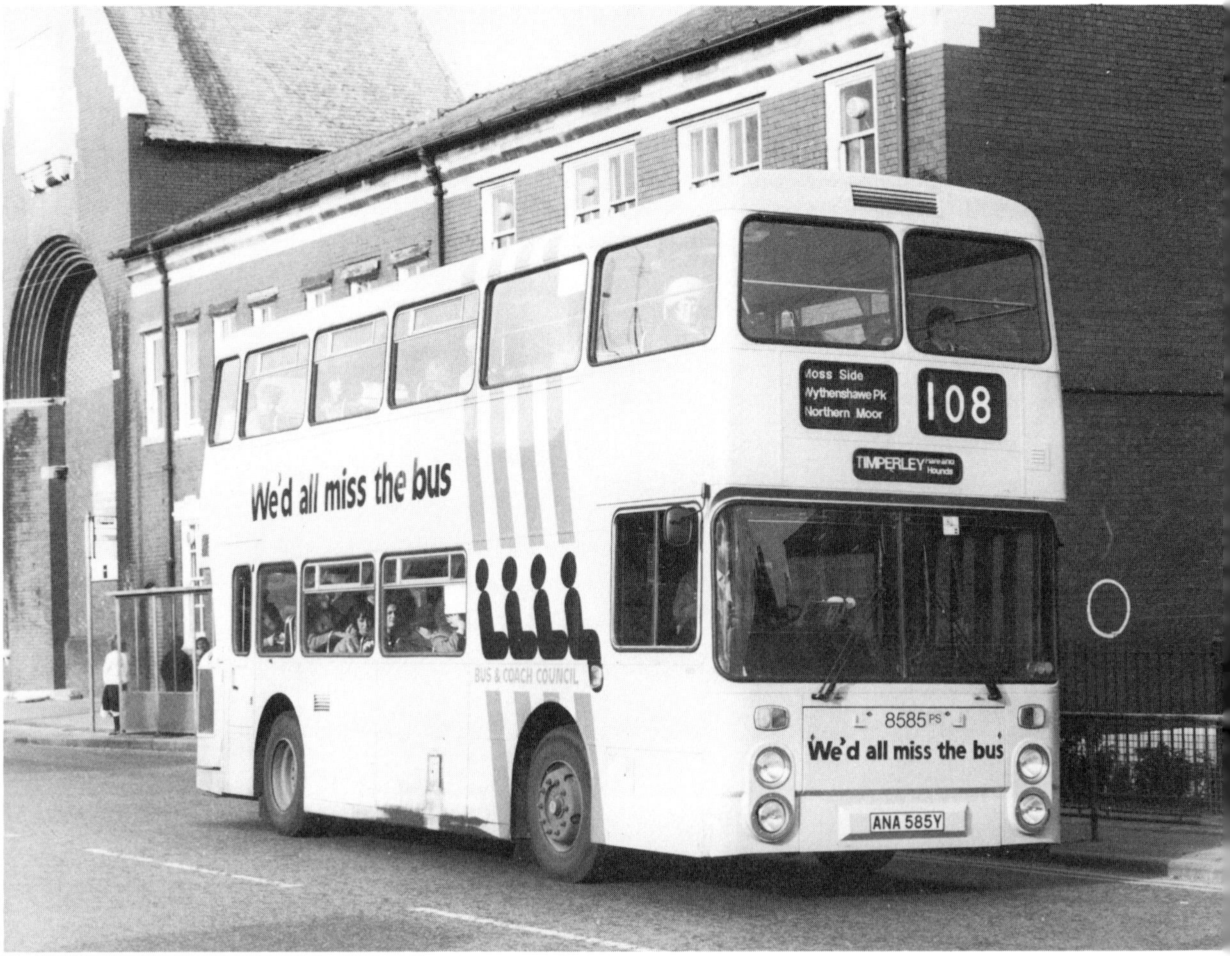

71
OLD TRAFFORD
mcw
ANA 175Y

Above: A pair of Scania BR112DH models with Northern Counties bodywork was bought for evaluation in 1983 and allocated to Leigh garage, which already had experience of the Metro-Scania single-decker, the entire fleet of 13 spending most of their careers there. No 1461, the first of the two, is depicted leaving Leigh bus station operating the Hindley Green Circular on 5 March 1984. *John Robinson*

Below: Greater Manchester Transport's coaching subsidiary, Godfrey Abbott, received this Duple Laser-bodied Leyland Tiger, No 52, in 1983, photographed heading along the A50 towards Knutsford on 3 April 1984, operating the daily contract for Barclays Bank at Radbroke Hall.   *John Robinson*

MERSEYSIDE PTE – CONSTITUENT FLEETS

Birkenhead

Below: Massey bodies were popular with Birkenhead Corporation; the first appeared in 1931, and the Wigan firm continued to be patronised until 1967, when it was taken over by neighbouring Northern Counties, which itself had supplied bodies to Birkenhead, albeit in smaller numbers than Massey, since 1934. Daimler CVG6 No 172, one of 15 bodied by Massey in 1949, stands in the rain at Woodside. These were the last new buses to carry the elaborate shaded lettering.
Roy Marshall

Bottom: Birkenhead was sufficiently impressed with its utility Guy Arabs to continue buying this model until 1956. No 235, photographed at Woodside in more favourable weather conditions, was one of 15 Mk IIIs placed in service in 1952. All were bodied by East Lancashire, the first time this firm had received orders from Birkenhead, apart from five replacement bodies constructed in 1942 for buses damaged in the blitz. On the right of the picture is No 386 (EBG 758), the last Guy Arab delivered to Birkenhead, also with East Lancashire bodywork, whilst all the other buses visible have Massey bodies. *Roy Marshall*

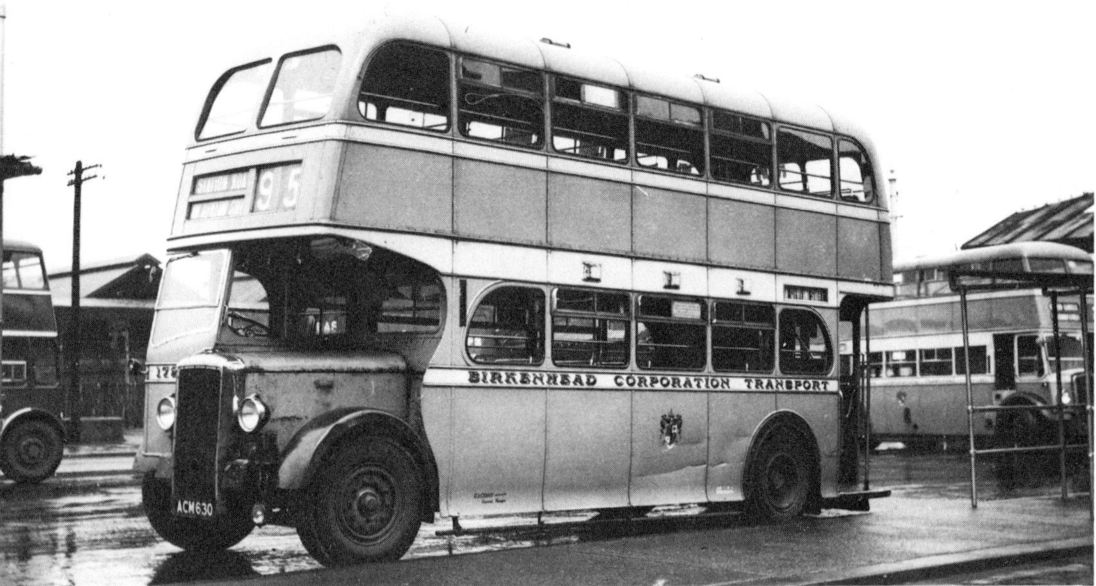

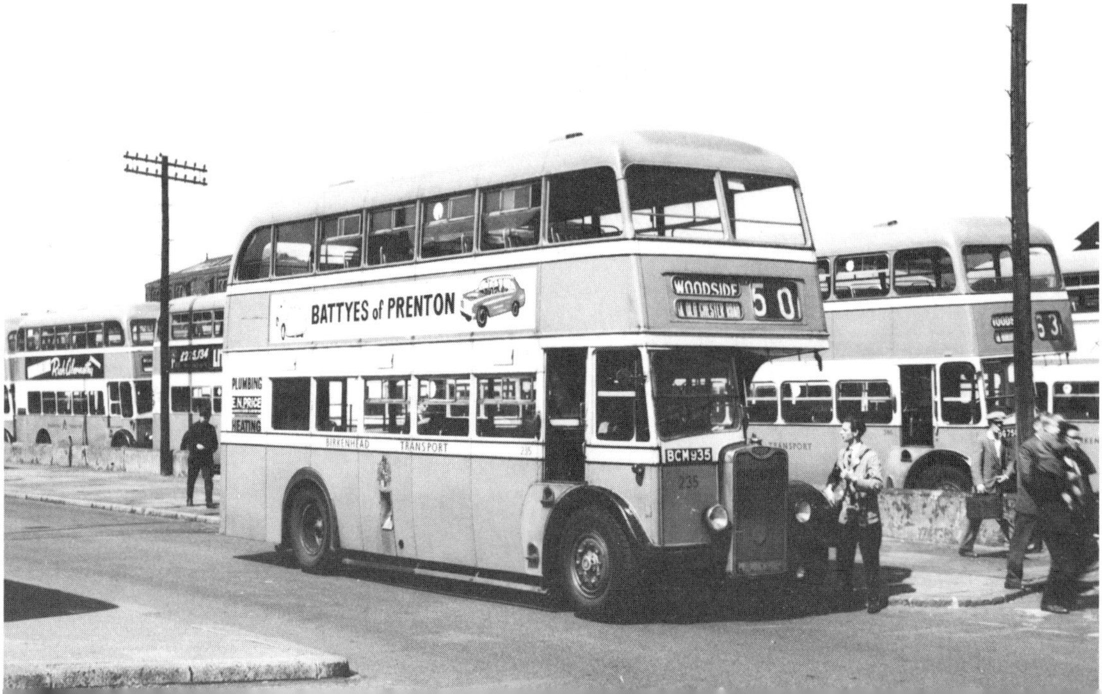

Top: Birkenhead looked to the local firm of Ashcroft to body five of the 1954 batch of 15 Leyland Titan PD2/12s. The pleasing appearance of these buses is conveyed in this view of No 268 (CBG 568).   *M. A. Taylor*

Above: Parked outside Laird Street garage, No 91 was the first of four Leyland Leopards with Massey bodywork new in 1964, which replaced Leyland Tigers, also with Massey bodies, new 16 years earlier.
Roy Marshall

Liverpool

Above: Representative of the early postwar AEC contingent in the Liverpool fleet, A319, seen arriving at Pier Head, was one of 42 AEC Regent IIs with Weymann bodies delivered in 1946-47. *Don Morris*

Left: Liverpool's C606-55 were specially modified Crossleys classed as DD42/7S, delivered in 1948-49. C632 stands at Pier Head before running out to Garston, ahead of A84 (NKD 584), one of 100 AEC Regent IIIs placed in service in 1953-55. All but two of these carried Crossley bodywork with full-width bonnets, incorporating Liverpool Corporation Passenger Transport-designed radiator grilles, which were produced and fitted by Crossley. A number of the bodies, including this one, were supplied as frames, panelled and finished by the Corporation at its Edge Lane works. *R. H. G. Simpson*

Above: In order to modernise its fleet in the early postwar years, Liverpool purchased large quantities of Weymann body shells for mounting on AEC and, to a lesser extent, Daimler chassis. Some were completed by outside contractors but the majority, including the one on this 1949 Daimler CVA6, were finished at Edge Lane works where this photograph of D585 was taken. *Merseyside PTE*

Below : Photographed passing St George's Hall as it heads south along Lime Street, Liverpool B2 was one of four Duple-bodied Bedford OBs acquired secondhand in October 1952 for operation on the airport service. *Robert F. Mack*

Right: Liverpool latterly used three different liveries; green and cream, cream and green, and aluminium and green, which were perpetuated by Merseyside PTE in its early years. 1959 AEC Regent V A232 carries the unpainted scheme in this 1969 view in Derby Square. This was another bus to carry a body completed by the Corporation at Edge Lane works, in this case on Metro-Cammell frames. Liverpool's second-generation new-look front-end, built on the chassis by AEC, comprised a more or less standard Regent V bonnet, but with a built-up nearside wing – incorporating the parking light – and a slatted radiator grille.
T. W. Moore

Below: The only AEC Bridgemaster with a major operator in the North Western Traffic Area was Liverpool's E3, which was built in 1958 as an AEC demonstrator. It was purchased in October 1959, after being on loan to a number of operators, including Liverpool Corporation. It is seen in Water Street on 25 August 1969, at the same spot as A319, but with the Corporation Tramways and the Liverpool Overhead Railway long since gone. *Roy Marshall*

Above: The Liverpool Corporation design of Metro-Cammell body first appeared on the city's streets in 1962, a total of 380 Leyland Atlanteans receiving them between then and 1967. L501 passes L754 in Derby Square, whilst a Crosville Bristol Lodekka loads in Lord Street.   *T. W. Moore*

Below: Amongst the last buses to be delivered to Liverpool were 25 Park Royal-bodied Bristol RELL6Gs in 1969, painted in a reversed version of the standard livery. Along with over 100 Leyland Panthers, these buses initiated Liverpool's OMO conversion. No 2014 is seen in Seaforth, with dock cranes dominating the skyline.   *Roy Marshall*

St Helens

Right: St Helens was the only municipal operator of trolleybuses in what is now Merseyside Metropolitan County, progressively converting its tramways to trolleybus operation between 1927 and 1936. In addition to the local services, St Helens' trolleybuses worked the through service to Atherton, which was operated jointly with the South Lancashire Transport Co until the route was converted to motorbus operation in November 1956. No 138 (DJ 6864) photographed in Baldwin Street on 27 August 1950 before heading out to Parr, was one of five Massey-bodied Ransome D4s placed in service in April 1936.
Roy Marshall

Below: Four Strachans-bodied Bristol K6As arrived in 1946. The last vehicle, No 50, was photographed outside Hall Street garage on 12 July 1953.
Roy Marshall

Above: The 7ft 6in wide 'tin-front' Leyland PD2/22 was one of the rarer Titan models, only a handful of operators specifying it. St Helens bought nine in 1954, which were fitted with East Lancashire 58-seat bodywork. Depicted at Southport's Ribble bus station, formerly Lord Street railway station until its closure in January 1952, is E86 (DDJ 493), awaiting departure for Warrington on service 319, which was operated jointly by St Helens Corporation, Ribble and Lancashire United Transport. *John Robinson collection*

Below: St Helens became an important customer of AEC after the war, purchasing complete RT-type Regent IIIs (the only operator outside London to do so), followed by Regent Vs, Reliances and, finally, Swifts. L37, a Metro-Cammell-bodied AEC Regent V from the penultimate batch of eight, new in 1962, leaves Liverpool for home on 5 March 1966.   *T. W. Moore*

Southport

Above: Southport placed in service a pair of Leyland Titan TD4s with locally-built Vulcan bodywork in 1936. One of these, No 50, is seen in Eastbank Street in postwar days. *M. A. Taylor*

Left: A number of utility Daimler CWA6s were placed in service between 1944 and 1946. Duple-bodied No 81 (EWM 550) is depicted arriving at Ainsdale Beach in glorious sunshine. *Robert F. Mack*

Above: Contenders for the most unusual buses in service with a municipal operator were Southport's ex-Army Bedford QL four-wheel-drive models. Twelve were purchased after the war, the top part of the cab being removed and an open-topped 24-seat bus body built in place of the original. No 1 (EWM 680), shown here, was the first conversion, and had a body built in the Corporation's own workshops, but most of the later ones had bodywork by a local concern, Rimmer, Harrison & Sutherland. In later years they were licensed as PSVs, enabling them to be used on public roads also. *Roy Marshall*

Below: Added to the Southport fleet in 1973 were 10 Leyland Atlantean AN68s with Alexander AL-type bodywork, of basically similar appearance to those operated by Merseyside PTE, which absorbed the resort's immaculate fleet the following year. No 85 is pictured heading along Lord Street for Woodvale on 27 October 1973. *John Robinson*

Wallasey

Left: Wallasey was a staunch supporter of Metro-Cammell, with the vast majority of its double-deck fleet being bodied by the Birmingham company from 1937 onwards. Leyland Titan PD1 No 32, seen in New Brighton, was one of a batch of 24 placed in service in 1948. *Don Morris*

Below: Wallasey was noteworthy in being the first operator to place a Leyland Atlantean in service. No 1 (FHF 451), fitted with Metro-Cammell body, took to the road in December 1958, and was followed by 29 similar vehicles delivered in three batches. Photographed at Seaview Road garage when new, it was restored to this condition by Merseyside PTE in 1983. *Roy Marshall*

Above: Photographed at Seacombe Ferry in 1963, No 33 was one of four Albion Nimbus with Strachans dual-purpose bodywork, seating 31, delivered the previous year. In addition to their intended role of one-man operation of lightly-trafficked services, they were also used on private hire duties from time to time. *Roy Marshall*

Below: The smallest bus to be operated by Wallasey was this 1960 Trojan 13-seater, purchased in 1963 from Banstead Coaches, Surrey, for use on a shopping service. Numbered 100, it is seen outside New Brighton station.   *Roy Marshall*

Merseyside Transport

Left: Amongst the orders inherited by Merseyside PTE on its formation was one for 125 33ft long Leyland Atlanteans with Alexander dual-doorway bodywork placed by Liverpool Corporation. The first of these, No 1111, was actually delivered to the Corporation in November 1969, but did not enter service until December when the PTE took over. Typical of these buses is No 1222, dating from 1971, which is depicted in Roe Street, Liverpool on 20 July 1979.
John Robinson

Below: Seen at the Vauxhall terminus of service 101 on 9 April 1984, No 2093 was a late survivor of the 10 Eastern Coach Works-bodied Bristol RESLs diverted from Potteries Motor Traction, which entered service in 1971. This service, marketed under the title of 'The Round-a-bout', was usually the province of Bristol LHSs or Dennis Lancets.   *John Robinson*

39
EASTHAM VILLAGE
3008
CKC 308L

Left: In 1973 a batch of 50 Metro-Cammell Weymann-bodied Daimler Fleetlines was purchased for allocation to the Wirral Division, where most of the existing vehicles were unsuitable for one-man operation. No 3008 is here in Chester Street, Birkenhead, just after leaving Woodside on 30 June that year, heading for Eastham Village.   *John Robinson*

Above: Photographed in Western Avenue, Speke on 9 April 1984, No 4046 was one of 60 Metropolitans (Scania BR111DH running units with Metro-Cammell Weymann bodywork) added to the fleet in 1974-75. *John Robinson*

Right: Nine Marshall-bodied AEC Swifts, ordered by St Helens Corporation, were delivered to the PTE in 1975, joining 63 similar vehicles already taken over from the undertaking. Amongst these was No 284 (GEM 604N) seen in Baldwin Street, St Helens on 21 June 1984. *John Robinson*

Below: Passing through Liverpool's Derby Square on 1 April 1983, en route from Halewood to Pier Head, No 0048 was one of 10 Dennis Dominators with distinctive Alexander R-type bodywork bought in 1982. *John Robinson*

Right: Merseyside PTE expanded its coach fleet considerably in 1982 with the addition of 12 Duple Dominant-bodied Leyland Tigers. Typical of these is No 7013, one of two allocated to Jackson Street garage, St Helens, where it is depicted on 5 March 1984. *John Robinson*

Below right: Ten Dennis Lancet midibuses with Duple Dominant 31-seat bus bodywork were added to the fleet in 1983. No 7023 stands at Edge Lane works on 9 May 1983, prior to entering service. *John Robinson*

0048
78 PIER HEAD
Merseyside Transport
DENNIS
CHF 348X

Private Hire
Leyland
CKC 624X

Merseyside
Transport
7023
7023
EKA 223Y
6106

National Bus Company Subsidiaries

Vehicles of the National Bus Company are familiar throughout the North Western Traffic Area. The two holding companies which were the forerunners of the NBC, BET Omnibus Services Ltd and Tilling Motor Services Ltd, registered in 1942 on the division of the Tilling & British Automobile Traction Co Ltd (TBAT), both had operating subsidiaries in the traffic area. These were Crosville Motor Services Ltd (under Tilling control), North Western Road Car Co Ltd (under BET control) and Ribble Motor Services Ltd (also under BET control). Ribble additionally had subsidiaries of its own in W. C. Standerwick Ltd and, later, Scout Motor Services Ltd, whilst North Western had subsidiaries in Altrincham Coachways Ltd and Melba Motors Ltd.

Prior to the break-up of TBAT in 1942 Crosville and North Western had been under the control of BET (British Electric Traction) and Tilling respectively. The exchange of 'parents' that year was reflected in the composition of the two fleets in the postwar years. Whilst Crosville had standardised almost exclusively on Leyland chassis from 1921 to 1942, when Tilling control began to dictate that Bristols be ordered instead, North Western found itself in very much the opposite situation. The company had standardised on Bristol chassis for buses since 1936 and continued to favour this marque until the supply was cut off following the nationalisation of Bristol in 1948, after which the number of buses bought from Leyland considerably increased.

In 1948 the Tilling group sold out to the British Transport Commission, which had been created by the 1947 Transport Act, and through this acquisition the BTC inherited a substantial manufacturing capacity in Bristol and Eastern Coach Works. Hitherto both concerns had sold their products to all comers, but the Transport Act prohibited the BTC from manufacturing for the open market, and henceforth the output of the two concerns was available only to the nationalised companies, with the result that their fleets became standardised on Eastern Coach Works-bodied Bristol buses and coaches. BET, however, held out strongly against nationalisation and maintained a much slacker lead on its subsidiaries, whose fleets were much more varied.

A period of comparative stability ensued until 1968 when BET agreed to the sale of its bus interests to the Transport Holding Company, the successor in 1963 to the BTC, whilst one of the consequences of the 1968 Transport Act was the setting up of the National Bus Company in 1969 to succeed the THC.

In January 1972, following a somewhat traumatic time for the company, the stage carriage services of North Western were divided between SELNEC PTE, Crosville Motor Services Ltd and Trent Motor Traction Co Ltd, along with the garages and vehicles to operate them. Trent, although based in the East Midland Traffic Area (outside the scope of this book) therefore gained an operating centre in the North Western Traffic Area, which thus warrants its inclusion.

Meanwhile, North Western remained in existence as a coach company, operating out of Manchester garage. In 1974 it was renamed National Travel (North West) and acquired the W. C. Standerwick fleet. Expansion followed in 1977 when the Birmingham-based National Travel (Midlands) was acquired, at which time the company was renamed National Travel (West), whilst in 1981 the Cheltenham and Bristol operations of National Travel (South West) were acquired. Under the NBC's reorganisation of coaching companies in 1984, whereby each was linked to a neighbouring bus company, the Northern operations of National Travel (West) became a coaching unit of Ribble, whilst the Southern operations at Cheltenham and Bristol became coaching units of Cheltenham & Gloucester Omnibus Co Ltd and Bristol Omnibus Co Ltd respectively.

Crosville

Right: Crosville MA619 (GJ 2007), photographed in Rhyl, was one of three 1930 AEC Regents with Eastern Coach Works convertible open-top bodywork acquired in 1950 from Brighton, Hove & District, which was a regular supplier of open-toppers to Tilling companies in postwar years. They entered service in 1951, painted in cream livery, joining two similar buses from the same source which had entered service the previous year. All five remained in service until 1954, after which they were sold for scrap.   *Robert F. Mack*

Below: Fourteen ex-Sheffield Corporation Cravens-bodied Leyland TDs were acquired in 1946, made up of TD3, TD3c and TD4c models. M504 (BWA 412), photographed near Rhyl, was one of the TD4cs, new as Sheffield No 212 in 1935. The torque converters on the gearless models (those suffixed 'c') were replaced by crash gearboxes before the buses entered service with Crosville. All but two of the batch were rebodied between 1950-52, most receiving second-hand bodies (from Crosville and Salford Corporation) but in 1952 three, including M504, were fitted with new bodies built by Crosville itself, which incorporated standee windows in the lower saloon.   *Don Morris*

Above: History repeated itself 34 years later when six East Lancashire-bodied Bristol VRs, new to Sheffield Corporation in 1972, were acquired from South Yorkshire PTE in 1980. HVG931, originally Sheffield No 267, is seen at work in Pwllheli in August 1982. *T. W. Moore*

Below: The Tilling group's standard single-decker in the immediate postwar years was the Bristol L-type, with 35-seat rear-entrance bodywork by Eastern Coach Works. Crosville operated examples of all three major models: the L6A (with an AEC 7.7litre engine), the L6B (with the Bristol AVW engine) and the L5G (with the Gardner 5LW engine). SLA87 (JFM 116), photographed against a background of Ls at Wrexham garage, was an L6A new in 1948. *Roy Marshall*

Above right: The Tilling Group's standard double-decker in the 1950s and 1960s was the Bristol Lodekka with Eastern Coach Works body, nearly 600 of which entered the Crosville fleet between 1953 and 1968. A late-surviving LD6G model was DLG881 (838 AFM), which was in its 20th year when photographed operating a local service out of Crewe bus station on 24 September 1977. *John Robinson*

Right: After Lincolnshire and Eastern Counties, Crosville was the largest operator of the Bristol SC4LK, building up a fleet of 55 buses and 24 coaches between 1957 and 1961, principally for operation in North Wales. These bus versions, SSG641 and SSG642, seen in Llandudno, were new in 1959. *John Robinson*

BEECH DRIVE
K11
CROSVILLE
838
AFM

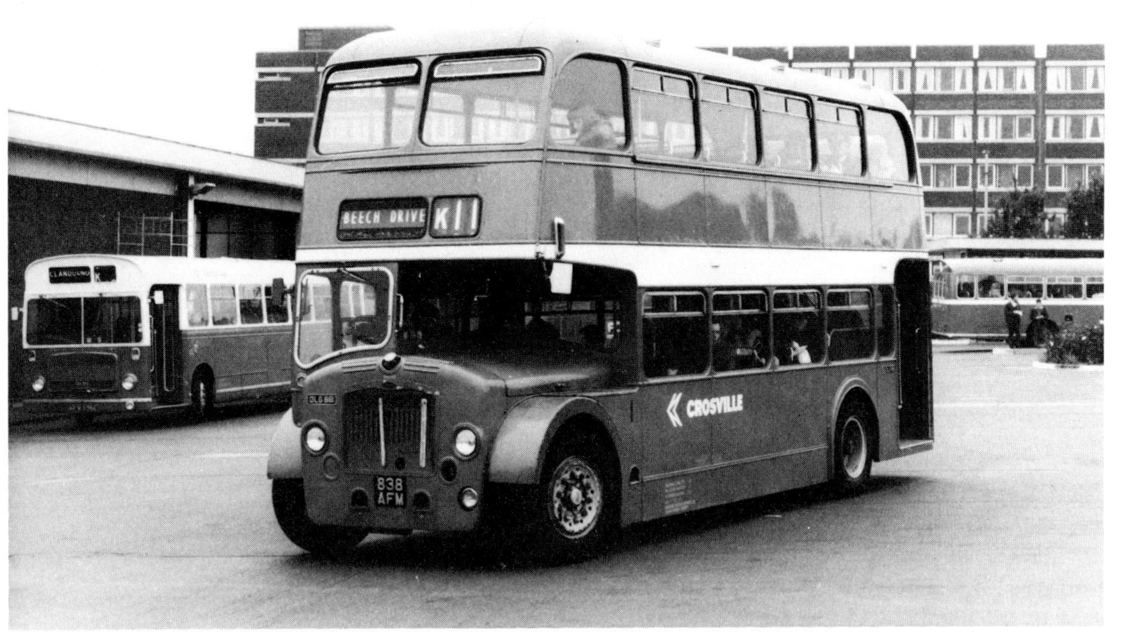

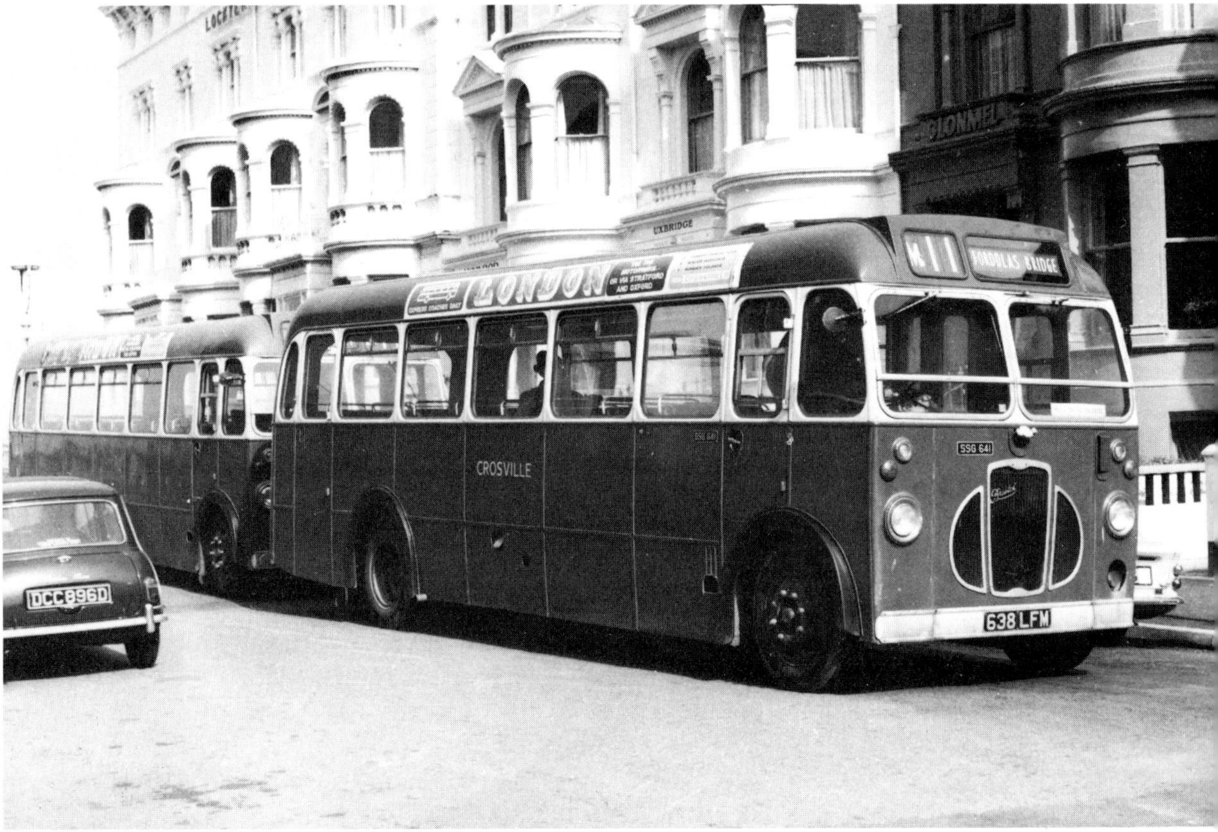
CLONMEL
UXBRIDGE
LONDON
CROSVILLE
638 LFM
DCC 896D

Above: Almost 240 Bristol MW6Gs with Eastern Coach Works bodywork were placed in service between 1958 and 1967. CMG561 was one of Crosville's penultimate batch of MW coaches and, despite being 10 years old, was in immaculate condition when photographed at Cheltenham coach station in July 1976.
T. W. Moore

Below: Amongst the vehicles which passed to Crosville on the division of North Western in January 1972 were the two Plaxton Panorama-bodied Leyland Leopards dating from 1963. CLL919, the second of the pair, was photographed in Lower Peover on 25 July 1974 before heading to nearby Radbroke Hall to work the Barclays Bank contract. *John Robinson*

National Travel West

Below: National Travel West operate a number of
Leyland Leopards fitted with distinctive Willowbrook
Spacecar bodywork. Typical of these is No 21, dating
from 1977, depicted leaving Preston bus station on 9
April 1984.   *John Robinson*

Bottom: Duple Dominant-bodied Leyland Leopard 34,
one of a batch of 15 placed in service in 1978-79, stands
in Liverpool's Hilbre Street coach station on 21 June
1984 before departing for London. On the left of the
picture is No 109 (ANA 109Y), one of five Leyland Tigers
with Plaxton Paramount 3500 bodywork delivered in
1983.   *John Robinson*

Top: The last Leyland Leopards added to the fleet were four PSU5E/4R models with Eastern Coach Works bodywork new in 1982-83 (Nos 91-94). No 91 was sold to Midland Red North after only seven months, but the others remained in service until September 1984, when they were sold to Eastern National. No 92 is depicted in Hotham Place, Liverpool, on 21 June 1984, shortly after the fleet had been taken over by Ribble, whose legal lettering it carries.   *John Robinson*

Above: Leaving Chorlton Street coach station, Manchester for London on 20 June 1984, No 105 was then the only survivor of a batch of five Leyland Tigers with Plaxton Paramount 3200 bodywork which were new the previous year (Nos 101-105). After only a few weeks with National Travel West four were transferred to other NBC subsidiaries in exchange for non-Rapide coaches, No 101 going to North Devon Ltd at Barnstaple and Nos 102-104 to Shamrock & Rambler at Bournemouth.   *John Robinson*

North Western

Above: North Western's first new Leylands were 25 Leyland Tiger TS1s with Leyland 26-seat bodywork delivered in 1929. No 395 (DB 5295) is seen on the Manchester to Hull limited stop service which was operated jointly with East Yorkshire, Yorkshire Woollen District and West Yorkshire. These buses had very short lives with North Western, all lasting only two years before being sold for further service elsewhere. *J. H. Fielder*

Below: Until the arrival of the Leylands, most new vehicles supplied to North Western had been Tilling-Stevens. This make continued to be purchased until 1932, however. No 473 was a B10A2, new in 1930 with a Tilling body, which was one of 133 Tillings rebodied by Eastern Counties in 1935 with bodywork to a design which became standard for North Western single-deck buses until 1940.   *W. J. Haynes*

Left: At the end of 1950 North Western embarked on an ambitious rebuilding programme, a total of 158 vehicles receiving new bodies after rehabilitation of the chassis at its Charles Street works in Stockport. One year into the programme it was the turn of the entire prewar Bristol double-deck fleet, totalling 64 K5Gs. No 422, depicted in Mersey Square, Stockport carrying its new Willowbrook body, was one of 24 K5Gs placed in service in 1938 with Eastern Coach Works bodywork.
R. H. G. Simpson

Right: AEC Reliances and Leyland Tiger Cubs were bought concurrently between 1954 and 1960 for both bus and coach applications. In 1957 six Albion Aberdonians, mechanically very similar to the Tiger Cubs, were additionally purchased but, despite the similarity, North Western was not influenced to become a repeat customer. All had Weymann bodywork to that concern's standard outline of the period. No 715 is seen at Lower Mosley Street bus station, Manchester alongside a Yorkshire Woollen District Leyland Tiger.
M. A. Taylor

Below right: North Western was the second largest user of the Dennis Loline, after Aldershot & District. 15 Mk IIs with East Lancashire bodies, new in 1960, were followed by 35 Mk IIIs bodied by Alexander in 1961-62. No 892, one of the 1962 intake, is seen parked in Great Bridgewater Street, Manchester, just across the road from Lower Mosley Street bus station. *Roy Marshall*

Below: North Western bought only 10 Leyland Titans with concealed radiators. One of these, No 669, leaves Parker Street bus station, Manchester, for Northwich when brand new in 1956. The lowbridge Weymann body was fitted to a PD2/21 chassis. *M. A. Taylor*

BUXTON 27
NORTH WESTERN
LDB 715
715
NORTH WESTERN

PARTINGTON WOOD LANE
NORTH WESTERN
RDB 892
NORTH WESTERN

Melba Motors

The last vertical-engined Bristols to enter the North Western fleet arrived in 1950. Amongst these was a batch of Windover-bodied L5G coaches, all 12 of which were transferred to the newly-acquired fleet of Melba Motors, Reddish, from 1958. No 287, photographed in Stockport's Mersey Square, remained in service until 1961. *R. H. G. Simpson*

Altrincham Coachways

Right: Also taken over in 1958 was Altrincham Coachways. Amongst vehicles transferred from the parent fleet was No 710, a 1957 Leyland Tiger Cub with Burlingham Seagull bodywork, photographed at New Brighton. Both fleets were painted in the blue and cream livery of Altrincham Coachways, and continued to display their previous fleetnames until 1967, when they were wound up. The Melba fleet reverted to North Western livery, whilst Altrincham Coachways was sold to Godfrey Abbott Tours, West Timperley, along with some coaches.
R. H. G. Simpson

Ribble

Below: Ribble had 27 Leyland Tiger TS7 chassis fitted with new Burlingham 35-seat bus bodies in 1949. Most had originally been coaches new in 1935-36 with English Electric bodywork but, additionally, 11 secondhand chassis were purchased, seven from Devon General and four from Yorkshire Woollen District. The original petrol engines were replaced by 7.4litre diesel engines on rebodying. No 219, photographed at Lower Mosley Street, Manchester before departing for Burnley, was one of the ex-Devon General vehicles dating from 1936, and remained in service with Ribble until 1961. *M. A. Taylor*

Bottom: Well-known in the Ribble fleet were the 50 Leyland Titan coaches, popularly dubbed 'White Ladies'. The first 30, introduced in 1949, had Burlingham bodywork of five-bay construction on PD1/3 chassis, whilst the remaining 20, placed in service the following year, had similar-looking bodies by East Lancashire, but with only four bays, mounted on PD2/3 chassis. Their lowbridge bodies seating 49 were air-conditioned and incorporated a twin sunshine roof, visible in this view of East Lancashire-bodied No 1232 (DCK 203) at Burnley, before departure for Manchester. *R. H. G. Simpson*

Right: From 1954 Ribble's standard single-deck chassis for both bus and coach applications was the Leyland Tiger Cub. No 951, photographed when new, was one of 15 PSUC1/2 models with Burlingham Seagull bodywork which entered service that year. *M. A. Taylor*

Below: Photographed at Lancaster bus station on the X40 Manchester-Keswick service, Leyland Atlantean No 1256 (NRN 605) was one of 37 'Gay Hostess' double-deck coaches delivered to Ribble and the associated Standerwick fleet between 1959 and 1961. The Weymann body contained only 50 seats (34 up, 16 down) and, as the advertisement on the side proclaims, air suspension was fitted, although this was later abandoned because of maintenance problems. Originally 15 of the Gay Hostesses were in the Ribble fleet and 22 were operated by Standerwick, but in 1963 11 of the Ribble vehicles were transferred to Standerwick and four to Scout, so concentrating all 37 coaches on the Lancashire-Birmingham-London services. *R. H. G. Simpson*

Left: The first of many Leyland Leopard coaches bought by Ribble were 35 with Harrington Cavalier bodywork which arrived in 1961. The penultimate vehicle of the batch, No 1052, is illustrated soon after entering service. *H. W. Peers*

Below: Sixteen Albion Lowlanders with full-fronted Alexander bodywork were delivered in two batches in 1964 and 1965, becoming the last front-engined buses to join the Ribble fleet. No 1864, from the final batch of six, stands in Moor Lane bus station, Bolton, before working service 313 to Chorley. *Roy Marshall*

Right: Ribble introduced a part-week service in 1978 linking a number of villages in the Ribble valley with Clitheroe, Nelson and Burnley. Initially the service was operated with a Seddon midibus hired from Greater Manchester Transport, but it popularity was such that two specially-built Bristol LHS models with Eastern Coach Works 35-seat bodywork measuring 26ft 6in × 7ft 6in were purchased in 1980. Allocated to Clitheroe garage, these vehicles officially recognised the name 'Betty's Bus' after the regular driver, Mrs Betty Gray, who is seen at the wheel of No 271 in Nelson bus station on 1 February 1984.   *John Robinson*

Below: Leyland Nationals are the predominant single-deck type in the current fleet, some 300 being operated. No 875, depicted in Market Street, Wigan on 10 December 1983, was one of 65 10.6m National 2 models added to the fleet in 1980-81. The overall advertising livery is for Ribble's travel agency service. *John Robinson*

Scout

Above: Following the Ribble takeover of Scout in 1961, a number of vehicles were transferred from the parent fleet, amongst them this all-Leyland Titan PD2/3, one of a large batch delivered to Ribble in 1948-49, which assumed fleetnumber S13 with Scout. It is seen leaving Starchhouse Square, Preston for Blackpool on 17 August 1963.   *Roy Marshall*

Left: Scout specified attractive Duple Donnington bodies for four Leyland Tiger Cubs and five Leyland Leopards, delivered in 1960 and 1961 respectively. The first of the Tiger Cubs is seen in Starchhouse Square carrying its post-takeover fleetnumber, S54, above the grille.   *M. A. Taylor*

Below left: Thirty-five Leyland Leopards with Plaxton Panorama 49-seat bodywork were delivered to Ribble and its subsidiary fleets in 1964. Typical of these is S739, one of the four allocated to Scout.   *R. H. G. Simpson*

Standerwick

Above right: W. C. Standerwick Ltd of Blackpool was purchased by Ribble in November 1932, remaining a subsidiary until 1974 when the fleet was transferred to the newly-formed National Travel (North West) company. Back in the late 1940s Standerwick had taken delivery of 48 Leyland Tiger PS1/1s with Burlingham coach bodywork including No 96, seen at Blackpool's Coliseum coach station in the summer of 1959 before departure for Birmingham.   *Roy Marshall*

Right: Amongst the 1951 deliveries to Standerwick were 10 Leyland Royal Tiger PSU1/15 coaches with Leyland bodywork, typified by No 131. The route details on the louvres over the side windows read 'BLACKPOOL BIRMINGHAM COVENTRY DUNSTABLE LONDON'. *Don Morris*

Below: Replacements for Standerwick's Gay Hostess Atlanteans were Bristol VRL/LH models with Eastern Coach Works 60-seat bodywork, a fleet of 30 entering service between 1968-72. Two examples, Nos 62 (OCK 62K) and 54 (LRN 54J), are seen in Pool Meadow, Coventry in 1971, making the first of their Midlands stops before continuing to Birmingham and the Northwest. *T. W. Moore*

Trent

Above left: On the division of North Western in 1972, the company's operations in the Buxton and Matlock areas were taken over by Trent, resulting in that company gaining an operating centre in the North Western Traffic Area in Buxton garage. A number of buses, all single-deck, were acquired with the garages. No 295, seen in Buxton bus station on 21 June 1975, dated from 1963 and was one of nine Leyland Leopards with Alexander Y-type bodywork taken over, joining a number of similar vehicles already in the Trent fleet. *John Robinson*

Left: Trent briefly turned to lightweight chassis in 1976 when it purchased eight Willowbrook-bodied Ford R1114 buses. The first, No 393, stands in Buxton bus station on 28 August 1976. *John Robinson*

Below: Originally No 259 in the Midland General fleet, which was placed under Trent control in 1972, this 1958 dual-purpose Bristol MW6G (28 DRB) was one of a handful subsequently transferred to the parent fleet. It is seen outside Buxton garage on 3 September 1973 wearing full Trent livery and carrying fleetnumber 168. *John Robinson*

Independents

Generally speaking, the North Western Traffic Area has not been fertile territory for independent bus operators since the late 1920s although, paradoxically, it was the home of Lancashire United Transport which was, on its absorption by Greater Manchester Passenger Transport Executive in 1981, the country's largest independent bus operator. LUT had very much the same image as the area agreement companies, even to the extent of having a trolleybus-operating subsidiary in the South Lancashire Transport Co.

Until the mid 1940s all British bus and coach operating companies, except the London Passenger Transport Board, were 'private enterprise' organisations and, therefore, any operator outside the municipalities could be considered independent. However, the distinction between the truly independent operator and these major companies lay in the area agreement system developed by the latter. This was an arrangement for deciding the extent to which neighbouring companies could extend their networks as they grew closer to each other, at the same time enabling operating boundaries to be drawn where rival organisations of similar strength met.

There were many more independent operators whose main business was bus operation in the past than now. Prior to World War 2 and, to a much lesser extent after it, area agreement companies had tended to buy out competing operators when the opportunity arose. For instance Ribble Motor Services, which commenced operations in 1919 by taking over the independent business of J. Hodson of Preston, rapidly grew through a policy of buying up numerous other independents in its chosen area. To the south of this area Crosville Motor Services, with its railway connection in the late 1920s was similarly enabled to assume a dominant position by purchasing.

The extent of independent bus operation has always varied considerably between different parts of the area. The conurbations of south and central Lancashire and north Cheshire were dominated by municipal operators from the turn of the century, leaving little potential traffic for the independents, although LUT managed to occupy virtually every space between the municipalities in south Lancashire.

In the Wrexham area conditions in the mid 1920s favoured the development of new bus services to locations not served by the established company, Wrexham District Tramways, later Western Transport. Independent bus operators grew by a succession of leaps and bounds and even now, over 50 years after Crosville took over Western Transport, Wrexham remains one of the principal pockets of independent bus operation in the North Western Traffic Area.

Elsewhere they are scattered, although a number of concerns, many of which are old-established, continue to operate in the area around Bangor, Caernarvon and Pwllheli. In the English part of the area the surviving bus-operating independents number a mere handful. J. Fishwick & Sons, the only survivor of the once numerous independent contingent to be found in the Preston area, has now assumed the position of the North Western Traffic Area's largest independent bus operator, its stage carriage activities being closely integrated with those of Ribble, which took over other well-known concerns such as Viking Motors, Scout Motor Services and Bamber Bridge Motor Services in the 1950s and 1960s. Another operator worthy of mention is A. Mayne & Son of Manchester, which survived all Manchester City Transport's attempts to buy it out, and still remains independent, and continues to operate stage-carriage services in the heart of Greater Manchesters PTE's area.

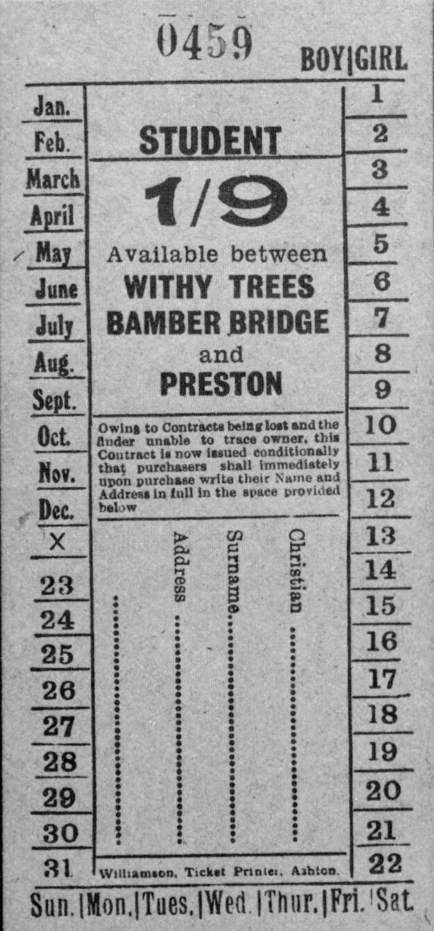
0459
BOY|GIRL
Jan.
Feb.
March
April
May
June
July
Aug.
Sept.
Oct.
Nov.
Dec.
X
23
24
25
26
27
28
29
30
31
STUDENT
1/9
Available between
WITHY TREES
BAMBER BRIDGE
and
PRESTON
Owing to Contracts being lost and the finder unable to trace owner, this Contract is now issued conditionally that purchasers shall immediately upon purchase write their Name and Address in full in the space provided below
Address
Surname
Christian
Williamson, Ticket Printer, Ashton.
1
2
3
4
5
6
7
8
9
10
11
12
13
14
15
16
17
18
19
20
21
22
Sun. | Mon. | Tues. | Wed. | Thur. | Fri. | Sat.

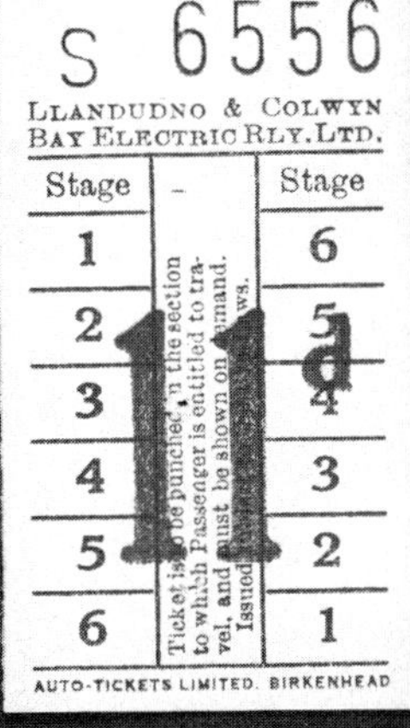
S 6556
LLANDUDNO & COLWYN BAY ELECTRIC RLY. LTD.
Stage
Stage
1
2
3
4
5
6
6
5
4
3
2
1
1d
Ticket is to be punched in the section to which Passenger is entitled to travel, and must be shown on demand. Issued subject to the Bye-laws.
AUTO-TICKETS LIMITED. BIRKENHEAD

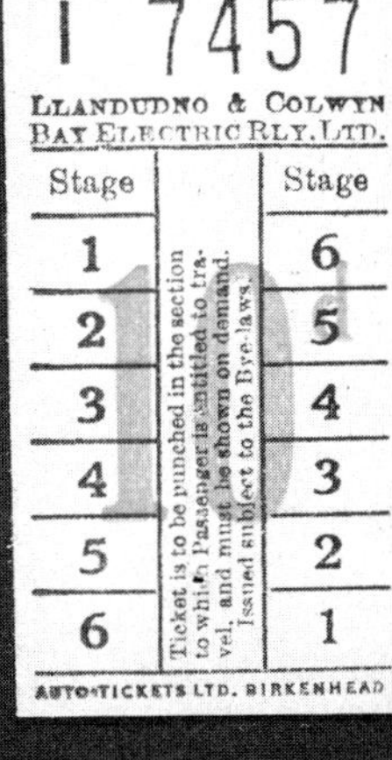
I 7457
LLANDUDNO & COLWYN BAY ELECTRIC RLY. LTD.
Stage
Stage
1
2
3
4
5
6
6
5
4
3
2
1
1d
Ticket is to be punched in the section to which Passenger is entitled to travel, and must be shown on demand. Issued subject to the Bye-laws.
AUTO-TICKETS LTD. BIRKENHEAD

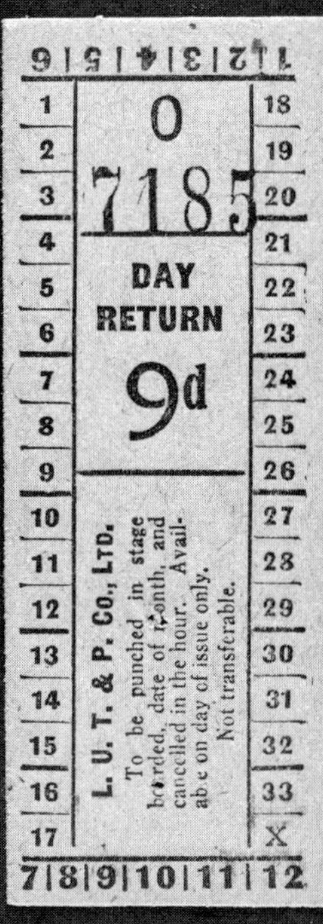
1|2|3|4|5|6
1
2
3
4
5
6
7
8
9
10
11
12
13
14
15
16
17
O
7185
DAY
RETURN
9d
18
19
20
21
22
23
24
25
26
27
28
29
30
31
32
33
X
L. U. T. & P. CO., LTD.
To be punched in stage boarded, date of month, and cancelled in the hour. Available on day of issue only. Not transferable.
7|8|9|10|11|12

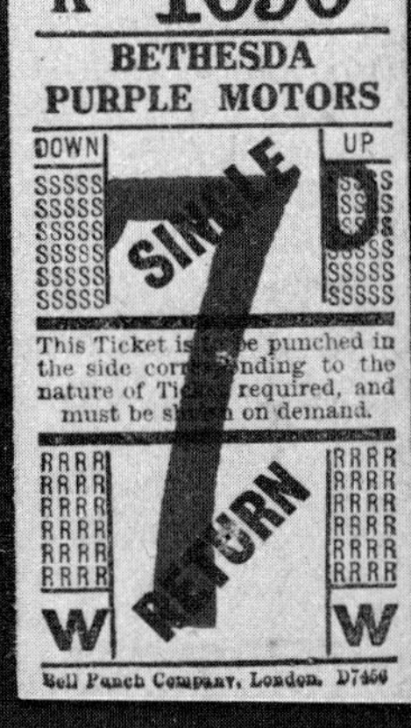
R 1690
BETHESDA
PURPLE MOTORS
DOWN
UP
SSSSS
SSSSS
SSSSS
SSSSS
SSSSS
SINGLE
7
RETURN
This Ticket is to be punched in the side corresponding to the nature of Ticket required, and must be shown on demand.
RRRR
RRRR
RRRR
RRRR
RRRR
W
W
Bell Punch Company, London. D7456

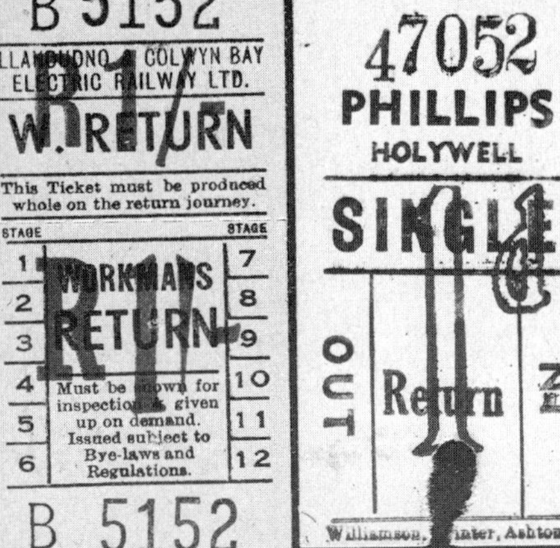
B 5152
LLANDUDNO & COLWYN BAY ELECTRIC RAILWAY LTD.
W. RETURN
1/-
This Ticket must be produced whole on the return journey.
STAGE
STAGE
1
2
3
4
5
6
7
8
9
10
11
12
WORKMANS
RETURN
R1/-
Must be shown for inspection, given up on demand. Issued subject to Bye-laws and Regulations.
B 5152

47052
PHILLIPS
HOLYWELL
SINGLE
6
OUT
Return
IN
Williamson, Printer, Ashton

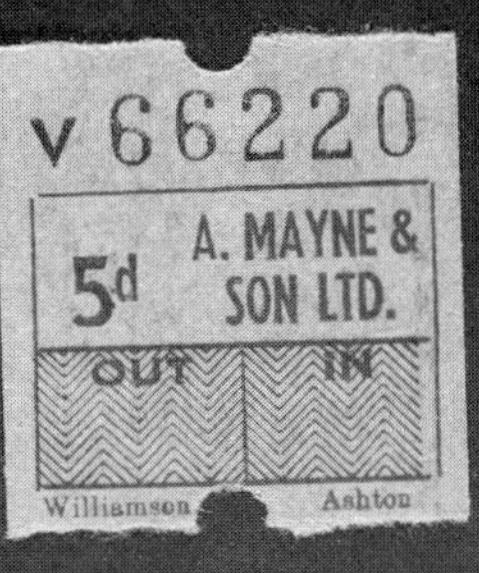
V 66220
5d
A. MAYNE & SON LTD.
OUT
IN
Williamson
Ashton

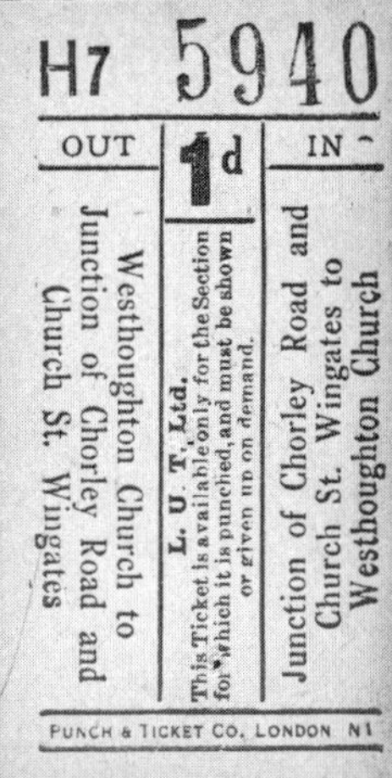
H7 5940
OUT
1d
IN
Westhoughton Church to Junction of Chorley Road and Church St. Wingates
L. U. T., Ltd.
This Ticket is available only for the Section for which it is punched, and must be shown or given up on demand.
Junction of Chorley Road and Church St. Wingates to Westhoughton Church
PUNCH & TICKET CO. LONDON N1

Lancashire United Transport

Above: Lancashire United was one of the few operators to purchase postwar Dennis Lances in any number, a total of 19 K2 models entering the fleet in the late 1940s. No 200 (GTE 868) from the first batch of nine, new in 1947, is seen in Southport on a private hire. Weymann 53-seat lowbridge bodywork was fitted, and the engine was the Gardner 6LW. *Roy Marshall*

Below: Single-deck rarities owned by Lancashire United included 40 Atkinson Alphas with bodies by various builders, which were placed in service between 1952 and 1955. No 531, fitted with Northern Counties central-entrance 'standee' bodywork, was the odd man out of the 1954 batch of 10, the remainder of which received Roe front-entrance bodywork. Depicted at Swinton garage, this bus was exhibited by Northern Counties at the 1954 Commercial Motor Show, and remained in service until 1966. *Roy Marshall*

Right: Lancashire United was an ardent supporter of the Guy Arab, purchasing over 360 of the model, starting with Arab I utilities in 1942, and gradually working through all the marks until the last Arab Vs entered service in 1967. No 103, a 1962 Arab IV with Northern Counties 73-seat bodywork, typifies LUT's standard double-decker of the period as it passes through Market Gate, Warrington, in October 1969, on one of the services operated jointly with Warrington Corporation. *T. W. Moore*

81
DAM LANE
NAVY STORES
103
567 TD

Above: Photographed leaving Arpley bus station, Warrington on 29 September 1973, also on service 81, No 204 was one of seven Marshall-bodied Leyland Leopards placed in service in 1965. *John Robinson*

Right: During its years of complete independence LUT purchased a total of 53 Daimler Fleetlines, all with Northern Counties bodywork. No 413, numerically the last of these, was one of 10 new in 1974, and is seen leaving Bolton bus station for Wigan on 30 July that year. Eighteen months later LUT became a wholly-owned subsidiary of Greater Manchester PTE, and all subsequent deliveries of new double-deckers comprised Leyland Fleetlines with Northern Counties bodies to the PTE's standard design, 90 such vehicles being placed in service between 1977 and 1980. Even when this picture was taken LUT's route numbers had been integrated within the Greater Manchester Transport series. *John Robinson*

Below right: Also placed in service in 1974 were 10 Bristol RESLs with Plaxton bodies incorporating coach seating in a Derwent shell. All were painted in an attractive reversed livery of grey with a red band, as displayed by No 419 passing Bolton market on its way to Eccles on 30 July 1974. *John Robinson*

South Lancashire Transport Co

Above: Photographed in Bolton in April 1936, No 48 was one of a number of Roe-bodied Leyland TTB4 six-wheel trolleybuses placed in service by Lancashire United's trolleybus-operating subsidiary, South Lancashire Transport Co, in the years 1935-38.
Leyland Vehicles

Left: A handful of utility Karrier W models were added to the fleet in 1943-44. No 63, fitted with Weymann bodywork, is seen approaching its Spinning Jenny Street, Leigh terminus in postwar days.
R. H. G. Simpson

Preston Area Independent Operators

Above: Preston was the meeting point for a number of independents, most of whose services terminated in Starchhouse Square, which has now disappeared under redevelopment. Scout Motor Services, whose head office and garage were located in the square, worked closely with its BET neighbour Ribble on a small group of local services in the Preston area, in addition to providing express services, principally between Blackpool and London and Excursions and Tours. Scout was, indeed, taken over by Ribble in December 1961, but continued to operate under its own fleetname, albeit using Ribble livery, until October 1968, when the routes .and vehicles were shared between Ribble and Standerwick. Leylands had for long been the principal make in the fleet, and two of Scout's Leyland Titan PD1s are seen in Starchhouse Square, with Bamber Bridge Motor Services No 1 (GTF 418), also a PD1, standing in the background. All three are fitted with lowbridge Leyland bodywork. *M. A. Taylor*

Below: Another view in Starchhouse Square, taken on 25 May 1952, showing two Scout vehicles and BBMS No 1 again. In the centre is Scout's Duple-bodied Daimler CWA6 of 1944 (No 19), whilst on the right is a 1941 unfrozen Leyland Titan TD7 with 53-seat lowbridge Leyland bodywork (ACK 529), originally intended for the Alexander fleet in Scotland, whose distinctive style of destination indicator is fitted. *Roy Marshall*

Right: Scout No 23, photographed in Talbot Road approaching Blackpool town centre, was one of five Leyland Titan PD3/4s new in 1958-59 with Burlingham bodywork essentially similar to Ribble's fully-fronted PD3/4s, but having half-cabs and Leyland's standard 'tin-front' bonnet. *R. H. G. Simpson*

Below right: A superb view of two classic buses, both all-Leyland Titans with lowbridge bodywork, in the erstwhile fleet of Bamber Bridge Motor Services, which was taken over by Ribble in 1967. On the left is PD1 No 1, appearing for the third time in this section, whilst along side is No 6 (ATD 776), a TD4 with Leyland's attractive 'V' front bodywork. *J. H. Fielder*

OUU
BLACKPOOL
Ty·Phoo TEA
Leyland
MCK 369
GAZETTE

BBMS
PRESTON
COOKSONS
MANCHESTER
BBMS
PRESTON
Mother you will feel much safer with MILLERS Milk
B.B.M.S.
ATD 776

Below: J. Fishwick & Sons of Leyland purchased a number of Weymann-bodied Leyland Olympics in the late 1950s. No 10 (MTD 514) is seen with a full load at the operator's Fox Street bus station in Preston on 21 March 1959, before setting off for Earnshaw Bridge.
Roy Marshall

Bottom: Fishwick's unique 1972 Fowler-bodied Leyland Atlantean photographed turning out of the main garage into Golden Hill Lane on 28 April 1976. This was the only double-deck body to be constructed by the Leyland-based concern, which was acquired by Fishwick in 1966, and built 12 bodies between 1968 and 1974, all but one for that operator. The chassis of No 6, a PDR1/3 model, had been purchased by Fishwick in 1969.
Roy Marshall

Right: Fishwick is the only UK operator of the AN69 variant of the Leyland Atlantean, two such vehicles being owned. No 2, the newer of the pair, carries Eastern Coach Works Olympian-style bodywork, and entered service early in 1984. It is depicted leaving Preston bus station for Leyland on 9 April 1984.   *John Robinson*

Below right: Viking Motors, Preston operated rural services in the Fylde to Great Eccleston area, together with excursions and tours, until it was acquired by Ribble in 1952. CRN 59, pictured in Preston's Starchhouse Square, was one of a pair of Daimler CVD6s with lowbridge Strachans bodywork new in 1949. Origianlly numbered 7, it was carrying fleetnumber 4 by the time this photograph was taken on 25 May 1952.
Roy Marshall

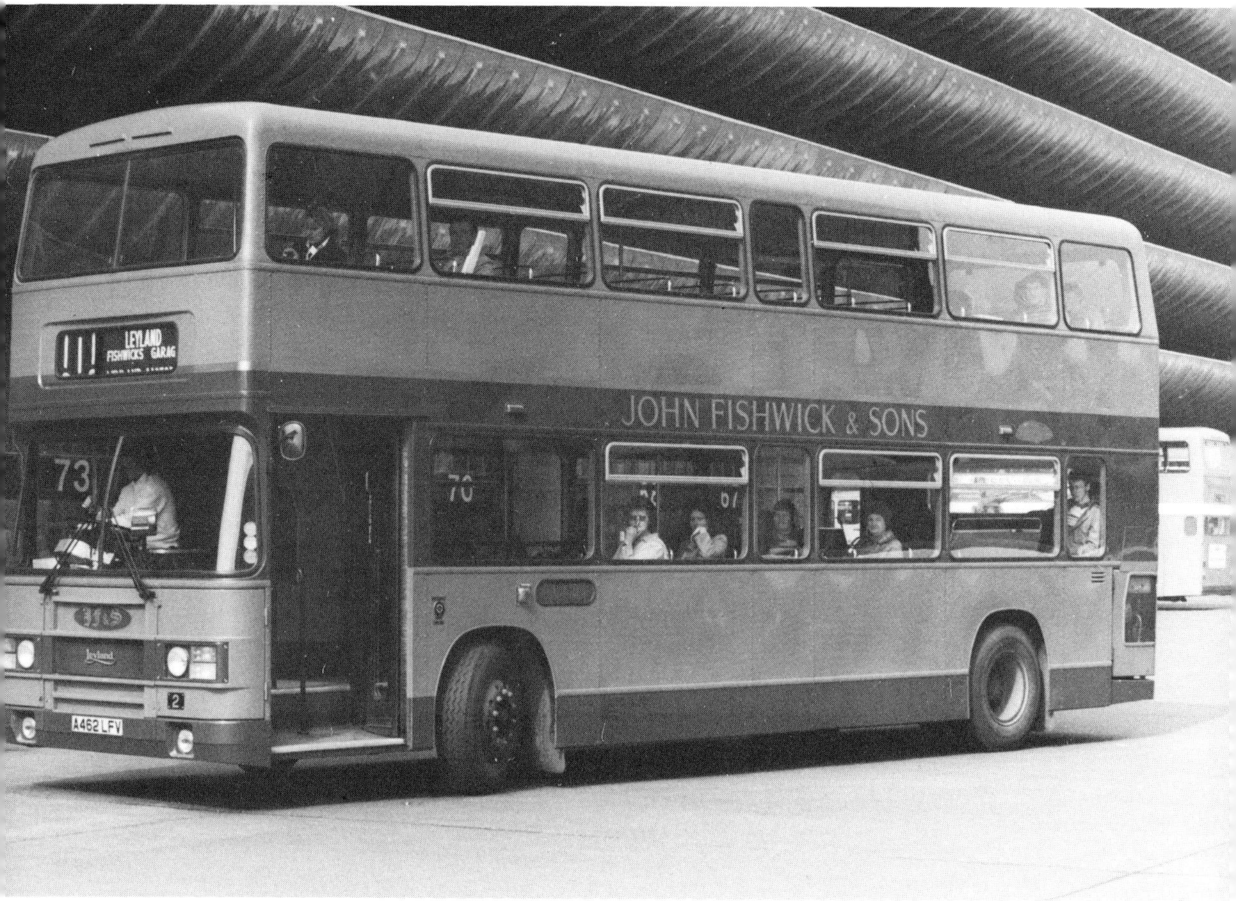
111
LEYLAND
FISHWICKS' GARAG
JOHN FISHWICK & SONS
73
A462 LFV

FOR SALE
VIA WOODPLUMPTON
CROSSE & BLACKWELL
SOUPS—NOURISH
CRN 59

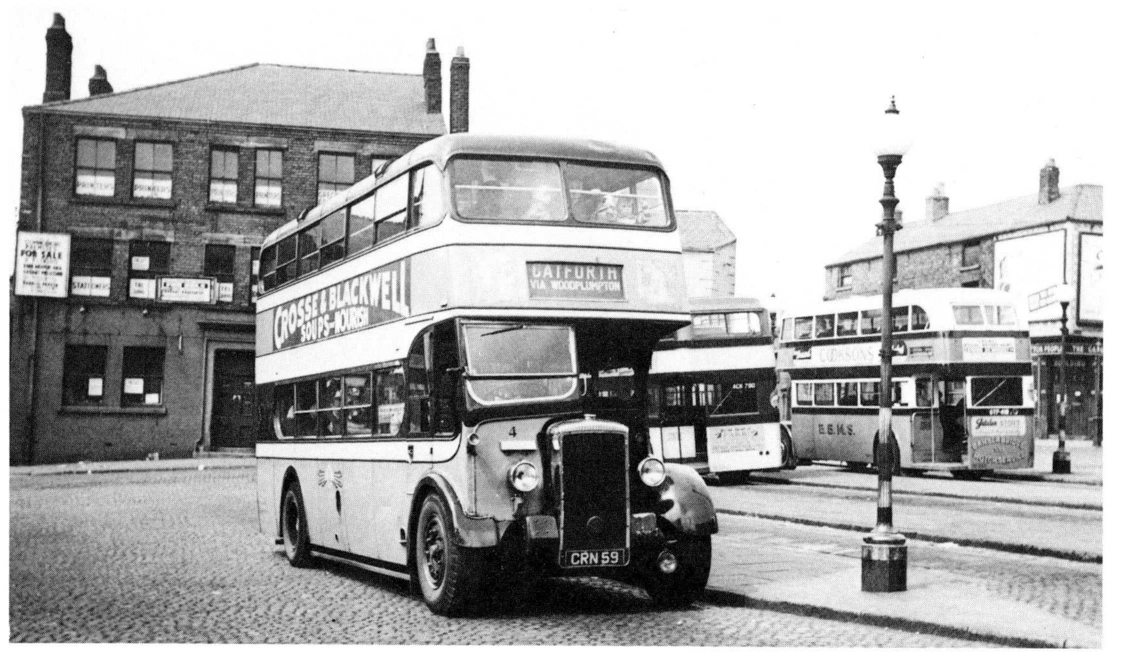

Other English Independent Operators

Below: Acquired from Hants & Dorset, this Eastern Coach Works-bodied Bristol LH6L of Derbyshire independent, Eric W. Bowers, Chapel-en-le-Frith is seen operating the weekdays only service from Chinley (Railway Station) to Chinley (Shallcross Estate) on 8 October 1980. *Roy Marshall*

Bottom: Charnock Richard operator A. Corless (t/a Corless Services) operated a Chorley-Wigan service. Seen in Wigan bus station on 22 March 1953 is his No 1 (GTJ 955), an all-Leyland Titan PD1 with lowbridge bodywork, which was bought new. *Roy Marshall*

Right: Another small Lancashire independent to buy a Leyland Titan new was Oliver Hart of Coppull, who used this PD2/1 model with highbridge Leyland bodywork, No 10 (JTC 912), on his Chorley-Southport service. *M. A. Taylor*

Below right: For many years A. Mayne & Son of Clayton, Manchester, favoured AEC Regents for its Ashton New Road services. This Park Royal-bodied Regent V, one of three new in 1961, is pictured in Manor Road, Clayton on 24 February 1976. Despite what the blind says, it is coming from Manchester and is heading for Droylsden, on what was by then Mayne's only stage carriage service. *John Robinson*

TARLETON
JTC 1

213 MANCHESTER
STEVENSON SQ.
DANISH
6972 ND

Mydel
CAR PARK
MAYNE
MAYNE
LRJ 213P
Mydel

BANK QUAY STATION
WARRINGTON
DANISH BUTTER
TINNED FRUIT
MILLINGS
GROCERS
AUSTIN
AND TRUCKS
NAYLORS
NMB 314

Left: The first rear-engined double-deckers in the fleet were five Roe-bodied Daimler Fleetlines which were placed in service in 1976. Typifying these is LRJ 213P seen heading out of Manchester along Great Ancoats Street, operating the Hartshead service which was introduced in 1979. *John Robinson*

Below left: A service from Warrington Bank Quay station to Appleton Thorn and Arley commenced in February 1943, jointly operated by Naylors Motor Services of Stockton Heath and Warrington Corporation Transport. Naylors' 1951 Guy Arab III, with lowbridge Massey bodywork, is seen unloading at Warrington's Bridge Foot in 1963. Naylors relinquished its licence for the service in December 1964, WCT assuming complete operation of the route. The Guy passed to WCT but was never operated, being sold for scrap shortly afterwards. *Roy Marshall*

Right: T. W. Pusill (t/a Suburban Motor Services), Penketh, operated services from Penketh and Great Sankey into Warrington. His first double-decker was this Leyland Titan TD4, purchased in 1936 in response to the growth in off-peak traffic. Two more TDs followed; all three carried Waveney bodywork, understood to be the only double-deck bodies constructed by the concern. No 5 (AED 435) ploughs through floods in Liverpool Road, Sankey Bridges, followed by one of the operator's Dennis-bodied Dennis Lancets. Suburban was taken over by Warrington Corporation Transport in February 1939; seven vehicles, comprising the three Titans, two Dennises, a Leyland Lion/Waveney and a Bedford WTB/Waveney passed to the Corporation for continued service. *John Robinson collection*

Below: Yelloway Motor Services of Rochdale became one of the country's leading independent operators of express coach services. Among the vehicles in the early postwar fleet was this Leyland Tiger PS2 dating from 1950-51 and fitted with locally-built Trans-United bodywork. *M. A. Taylor*

Above: For some years the Yelloway fleet consisted exclusively of AEC Reliances. Typical of those placed in service in the latter half of the 1960s is Plaxton Panorama-bodied KDK 801F, depicted in Derby bus station on 14 August 1976.   *John Robinson*

Right: Representing the current Yelloway choice of coach is A67 GBN, a Leyland Tiger with Plaxton Paramount 3500 bodywork, new in June 1984. It is shown passing Knutsford services on the M6 as it heads for the West Country on 14 October 1984.
John Robinson

Wrexham Area Independent Operators

Above: Leaving Wrexham bus station for Moss on 20 May 1961, GUE 249 was a Northern Coachbuilders-bodied Leyland Tiger PS1 operated by Chaloner, Moss, but new to Stratford Blue in 1948. *Roy Marshall*

Below: Edwards, Bwlchgwyn, acquired this 1963 Plaxton-bodied Bedford SB5 from Barfoot, Southampton, in 1971. It is seen leaving Wrexham on 19 April 1976 on the return working of the operator's Monday, Thursday and Saturdays only service from Llanarmon to Wrexham. *Roy Marshall*

Above: A Bedford OWB with Duple utility bodywork of M. A. Evans & Son, Wrexham, turns into Wrexham bus station in June 1956, operating the Rhosnessney-Wrexham service.   *Roy Marshall*

Below: A Duple-bodied Bedford SB of Phillips, Rhostyllen, photographed at Wrexham bus station on 16 August 1966. This operator ceased operation in 1978 and its two services, Tainant-Wrexham and Rhos-Wrexham, were taken over by Crosville Motor Services.   *Roy Marshall*

Above: T. M. R. & R. Roberts (t/a Vale of Llangollen Tours), Cefn Mawr, was the initial operator of the ex-Walsall 1968 36ft-long Daimler Fleetline, fitted with Northern Counties bodywork, after its disposal by West Midlands PTE. This unique vehicle is seen on a private hire in Llangollen on 7 September 1976, shortly after acquisition. Along side is 211 JUS, a Park Royal-bodied AEC Renown purchased from Barton, but new to Smith, Barrhead, in 1963. *John Robinson*

Above left: Williams, Ponciau, bought UKH 170W, a Bedford YMT with the first Plaxton Bustler body, after it had spent some time as a demonstrator for the bodybuilder. In this view, taken on 31 August 1983, it is depicted leaving Wrexham on the Rhos service. *John Robinson*

Left: The ex-Bury Guy Wulfrunian spent some time with Wright's, Penycae, towards the end of the 1960s. It is observed leaving Wrexham bus station on the operator's principal service, followed by Crosville Bristol LL6B SLB278 (NFM 34). *Roy Marshall*

make a DATE with the DAUPHINE
Sentinel
JWF 176

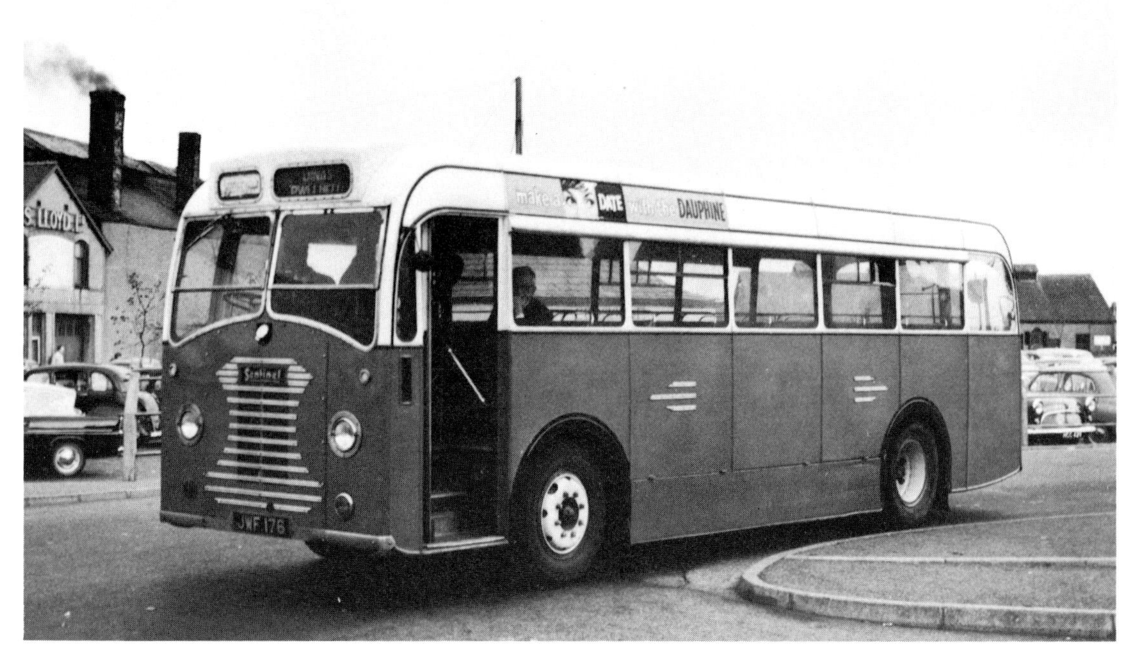

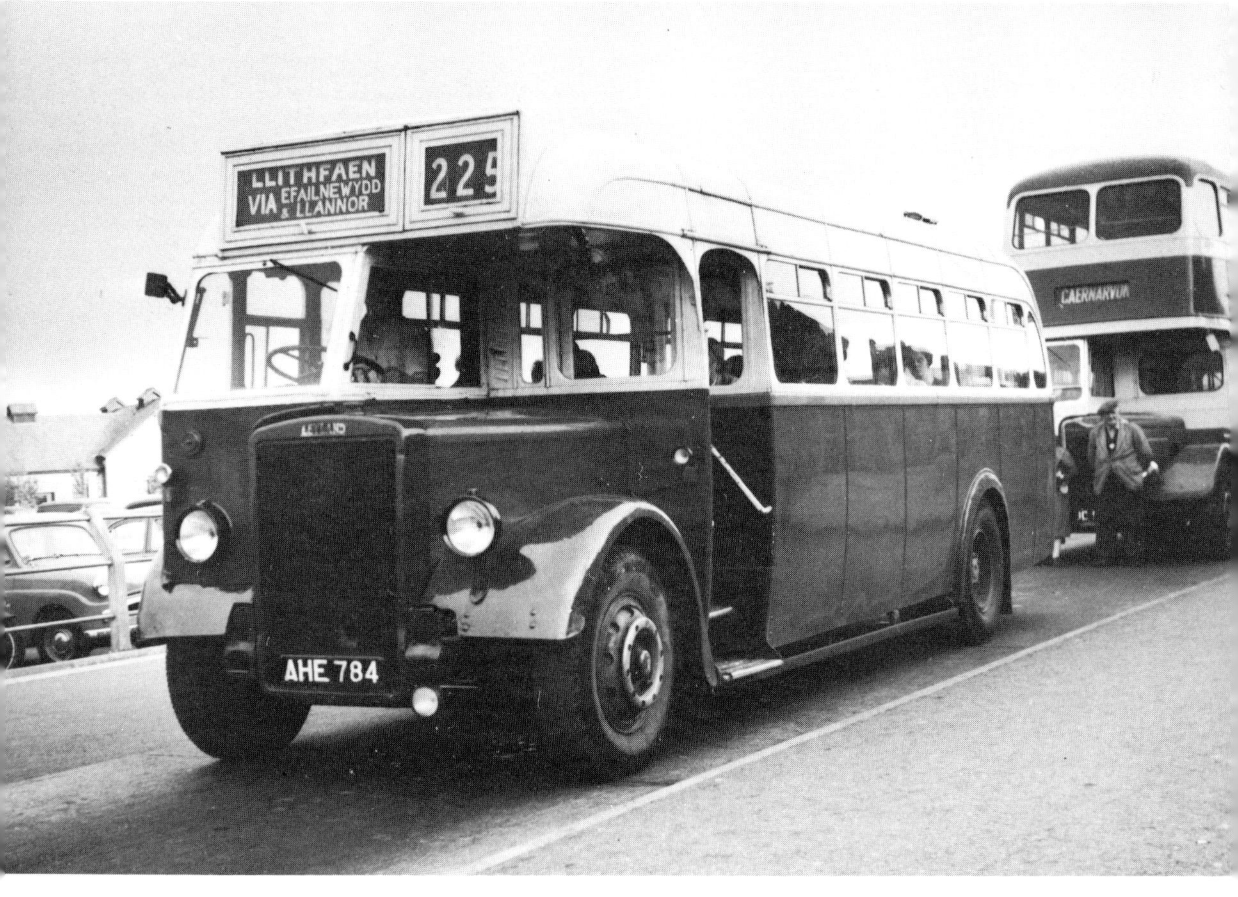

LLITHFAEN
VIA EFAILNEWYDD & LLANNOR
225
CAERNARVON
AHE 784

Caernarvon Independent Operators

Above left: T. H. Jones (t/a Caelloi Motors), Pwllheli, operated this Sentinal JWF 176 in the early 1960s. Photographed in Pwllheli on 24 June 1961, this unusual vehicle was new to Yorkshire operator Connor & Graham of Easington. *Roy Marshall*

Left: Williams, Llithfaen, Pwllheli, acquired this Roe-bodied Leyland Tiger PS1 from Yorkshire Traction. It is seen in Pwllheli on the Llithfaen service, with Clynnog and Trevor's Barnard-bodied Guy Arab, bought new, working that operators principal service, Pwllheli-Caernarvon, behind. *Roy Marshall*

Above: A later Clynnog & Trevor bus leaving Pwllheli for Caernarvon in August 1982 was 276 UVO, a 1964 Willowbrook-bodied AEC Reliance, new to East Midland. It was acquired along with sister vehicle 277 UVO in 1976. *T. W. Moore*

Below: R. H. Jones (t/a Express Motors), Tyddyn Canol, Rhostryfan, operated these two Burlingham-bodied Leyland Tiger TS8s, new to Ribble in 1939 (RN 8743 and RN 8781). In this view at Caernarvon Castle, taken in June 1956, a Commer Commando (JC 9920) belonging to the same operator is also depicted. *Roy Marshall*

Above: BJA 408, seen in Caernarvon on 4 June 1966 in service with E. W. Thomas (t/a Silver Star Motors), Upper Llandwrog, was a Bristol L5G, new to North Western in 1946. Originally fitted with Brush bodywork, it was one of 14 similar buses given 1948 Weymann bodies in 1957, which were previously fitted to prewar Leyland Tiger chassis. *Roy Marshall*

Below: Williams (Whiteways) of Waenfawr, operator of a number of services in the Caernarvon area, was a keen supporter of the Bedford OB. Two such vehicles are photographed in Manchester on a private hire; FF 5346 nearer the camera is fitted with a Duple Hendon body, whilst JC 9712 carries the far more common Duple Vista type. *M. A. Taylor*

Right: Jones & Davies of Deiniolen bought this all-Crossley DD42/7 in 1949. Seen in Bangor 10 years later, JC 9795 was a rare example of this type of bus being bought new by an independent operator. *Roy Marshall*

Below right: E. R. Pritchard (t/a Purple Motors), Bethesda, was one of countless independents to buy ex-London Transport Daimler Fleetlines in the early 1980s. Park Royal-bodied MLK 670L, here arriving in Bangor from Bethesda in August 1982, draws up alongside Crosville SNL651, one of the company's large fleet of Leyland National B-types. *T. W. Moore*

JC 9795

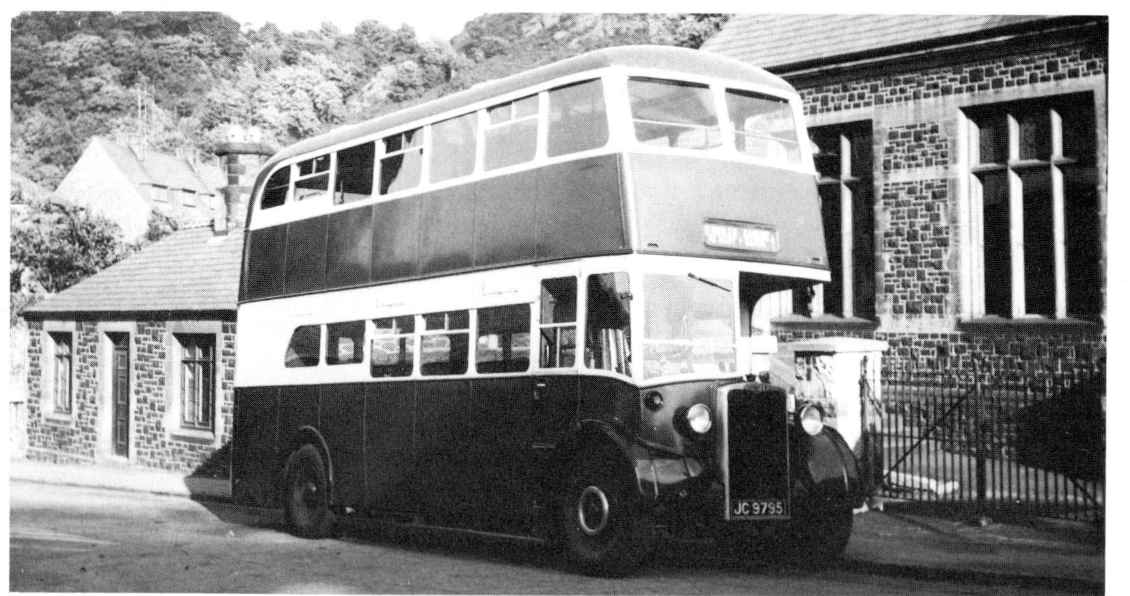

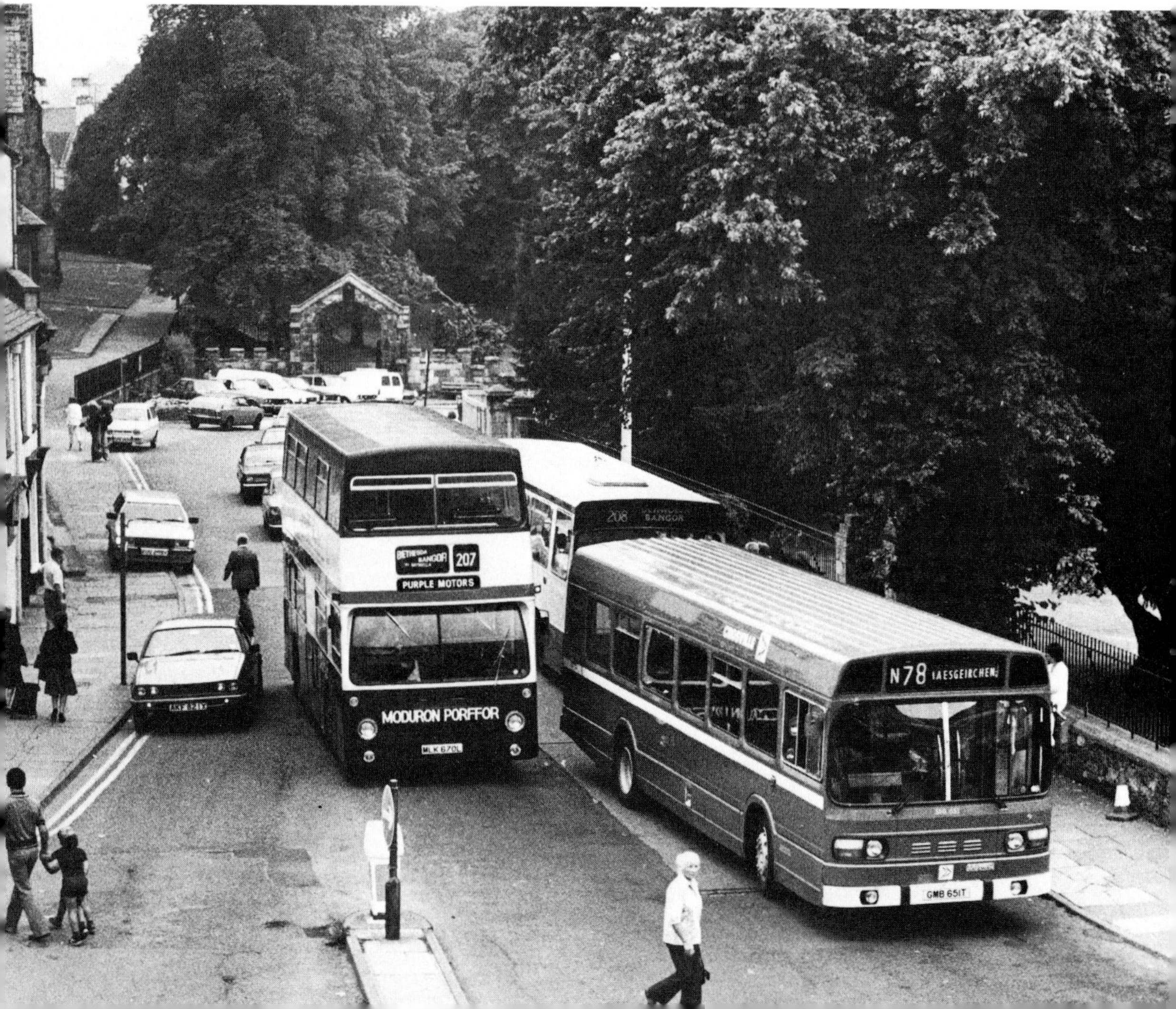
BANGOR
207
PURPLE MOTORS
MODURON PORFFOR
MLK 670L
208
BANGOR
N78
GMB 651T

Right: A former Hants & Sussex Duple-bodied Bedford
OB, GOU 888, in the fleet of Penmaenmawr Motor Co
stands outside the operator's garage on 8 June 1956.
Roy Marshall

Below: The Llandudno & Colwyn Bay Electric Railway
Ltd, which operated an electric tramway between the
two towns in its title, switched to motorbus operation in
March 1956, using a fleet of second-hand
double-deckers, predominantly Guy Arab IIs. No 12,
photographed leaving Llandudno, was a 1945
Weymann-bodied example, one of a number purchased
from Southdown Motor Services. Bus operation was a
brief venture, the company selling out to Crosville in
1961.   *R. H. G. Simpson*

Other Welsh Independent Operators

Above: After an absence of many years, the double-decker reappeared in the fleet of Bryn Melyn Motor Services, Llangollen, in 1982 when this 1967 Alexander-bodied Daimler Fleetline was placed in service. New to Alexander (Midland), its blue and cream livery closely matched that of its new owner, so no repaint was necessary. It is seen in Oswestry on 31 August 1983 after arriving on the service from Llangollen. Alongside is 947 JWD, a 1964 Plaxton-bodied Bedford SB5 of Fisher, Bronington, Flint. *John Robinson*

Below: A much earlier vehicle operated by Fisher was this Brockhouse-bodied Crossley SD42, depicted at Whitchurch bus station on 27 June 1959. *Roy Marshall*

LLOYDS
COURTAULDS
GREEN FIELD
Lloyds
FDM 568
SHREWSBURY
HB 7164
HIGH SPEED
TYRES LIMITED
TYRE
RETREAD
SERVICE
COLE L
EP 958

Left: P. & O. Lloyd, Bagillt, Flint, operated a number of contract services to Courtaulds' Greenfield works. Amongst the buses used was this Massey-bodied Foden PVD6 bought new in 1949. A similar bus joined the neighbouring fleet of Phillips, Holywell, the same year. *Roy Marshall*

Below left: Mid-Wales Motorways of Newtown, Montgomery, one of the southernmost operators in the North Western Traffic Area, ran this 1951 Dennis Lancet with D. J. Davies bodywork. It was one of four, new to Merthyr Tydfil Corporation, which were purchased in 1962, and is seen in Shrewsbury on 28 July that year. *Roy Marshall*

Above: Several independents had a policy of using vehicles of 'coach' character, even on bus services. A typical example is this Burlingham-bodied Foden PVSC6 owned by E. G. Peters, Llanarmon-yn-Ial, Denbigh, which is seen in Mold on 27 June 1959, before departing for its home village. *Roy Marshall*

Below: Phillips Motor Services, Holywell, Flint, owned this unusual Seddon-bodied Seddon Mark IV, depicted at Holywell on 2 January 1961, on the operator's Holywell-Mold service. *Roy Marshall*

Photographed in Llangefni on 29 May 1980, operating the Thursdays only Newborough-Llangefni service of Anglesey operator, Pritchard, Newborough, is 214 STD, a 1960 Yeates Europa-bodied Bedford SB1, acquired from Milburn, Benllech Bay in 1969.
Roy Marshall